Cambridge Primary

# Ready to Go Lessons for English

Step-by-step
lesson plans for
Cambridge Primary

## Stage 3

**Emily Budinger**

**Series editor: Emily Budinger**

**HODDER**
EDUCATION
AN HACHETTE UK COMPANY

The Publishers would like to thank the following for permission to reproduce copyright material:

**Acknowledgements**
**p.8ff:** Anne Fine, lesson based on *The Diary of a Killer Cat* (Hamish Hamilton, 1994), text copyright © Anne Fine, 1994;
**p.52:** Allan Ahlberg, 'Scissors' from *Please Mrs Butler* (Kestrel Books, 1983), copyright © Allan Ahlberg, 1983, reproduced by permission of Penguin Books; Valerie Bloom, 'Water Everywhere' from *Read Me 2. A Poem For Every Day Of The Year*, edited by Gaby Morgan (Macmillan Children's Books, 1999), reproduced by permission of Eddison Pearson; **p.55:** Kenn Nesbitt, 'My Senses All are Backward' from *The Aiens Have Landed At Our School!* (Meadowbrook Press), copyright © Kenn Nesbitt 2001. All Rights Reserved, reprinted by permission of the author; **p.58:** 'We're going on a turkey hunt', adapted from Michael Rosen, *We're Going on a Bear Hunt* (Walker Books, 1989), reproduced by permission of the publisher; **p.60:** Roald Dahl, extract from 'Meet the Muggle-Wumps' from *The Twits: Plays for Children*, adapted by Charles Wood (Puffin Books, 2003), text copyright © Roald Dahl, Nominee Ltd and David Wood, 2003, reproduced by permission of David Higham and Penguin Group USA; **pp.69–72:** *The Three Sisters*, reproduced by permission of East of England Broadband Network (E2BN); **p.76:** George Bird Grinnell, 'Two Fast Runners' from *Blackfeet Indian Stories* (BiblioBazaar, 2007); **pp.81–83:** Marcia Williams, lesson featuring *Greek Myths* (Walker Books, 2006); **p.98:** Emily Gravett, lesson based on *Meerkat Mail* (Macmillan Children's Books, 2007), copyright © Macmillan Children's Books 2007, by permission of Macmillan Children's Books, London, UK; **p.120:** Monica Gunning, 'Classes Under the Trees' from *Poems About School (Wayland Poetry Collections)* (Hodder Wayland, 1999); W. Les Russell, 'Red' from *Inside Black Australia: An Anthology of Aboriginal Poetry*, edited by K. Gilbert (Penguin Australia, 1988); **p.123:** A.B. Paterson, 'Old Man Platypus' from *The Animals Noah Forgot* (1933); **p.124:** Debjani Chatterjee, 'My Sari' from *Unzip Your Lips: 100 Poems to Read Aloud* (Macmillan Children's Books, 1998), reprinted by permission of the author; **pp.138–143:** Anthony Browne, lessons based on *Into the Forest* (Walker Books, 2005), copyright © 2004 Anthony Browne, reproduced by permission of Walker Books Ltd, London SE11 5HJ, www.walker.co.uk; **p.147:** Anthony Browne, text from *The Tunnel* (Walker Books, 1992), © 1989 Anthony Browne, reproduced by permission of Walker Books Ltd, London SE11 5HJ, www.walker.co.uk; **p.151:** Anthony Browne, adapted version of text from *The Tunnel* (Walker Books, 1992) © 1989 Anthony Browne, reproduced by permission of Walker Books Ltd, London SE11 5HU, www.walker.co.uk; **p.177:** Judith Nicholls, 'Explosive Tale', © Judith Nicholls 2012, reproduced by permission of the author; John Kitching, 'Family Problems' from *The Works*, edited / chosen by Paul Cookson (Macmillan Children's Books, 2000), reproduced by permission of John Kitching; Michael Rosen, 'A Young Man with Wobbly Eyes' from *Michael Rosen's Book of Nonsense*, © 1997 McDonald Young Books, reprinted by permission of Peters Fraser & Dunlop (www.petersfraserdunlop.com) on behalf of Michael Rosen; **p.178:** Kenn Nesbitt, 'A Shark is a Pet', copyright © 2012 Kenn Nesbitt. All Rights Reserved, reprinted by permission of the author; Kenn Nesbitt, 'My Elephant Thinks I'm Wonderful' from http://www.poetry4kids.com/poem-221.html1~UA_IhIFvOE, reproduced by permission of the author. All rights Reserved; **p.180:** Libby Houston, 'Shop Chat' from *Cover of Darkness, Selected Poems 1961–1998* (Slow Dancer Press, 1999), reprinted by permission of the author; Colin West, 'Toboggan', reprinted with permission of Colin West; **pp.183–184:** Trevor Millum, 'The Dark Avenger' from *The Works*, edited / chosen by Paul Cookson (Macmillan Children's Books, 2000), reprinted by permission of the author.

Permission for reuse of all © Crown copyright information is granted under the terms of the Open Government Licence (OGL).

Every effort has been made to trace all copyright holders, but if any have been inadvertently overlooked the Publishers will be pleased to make the necessary arrangements at the first opportunity.

Although every effort has been made to ensure that website addresses are correct at time of going to press, Hodder Education cannot be held responsible for the content of any website mentioned in this book. It is sometimes possible to find a relocated web page by typing in the address of the home page for a website in the URL window of your browser. Websites included in this text have not been reviewed as part of the Cambridge endorsement process.

Hachette UK's policy is to use papers that are natural, renewable and recyclable products and made from wood grown in sustainable forests. The logging and manufacturing processes are expected to conform to the environmental regulations of the country of origin.

Orders: please contact Bookpoint Ltd, 130 Milton Park, Abingdon, Oxon OX14 4SB. Telephone: (44) 01235 827720. Fax: (44) 01235 400454. Lines are open 9.00–5.00, Monday to Saturday, with a 24-hour message answering service. Visit our website at www.hoddereducation.com.

© Emily Budinger 2013
First published in 2013 by
Hodder Education,
An Hachette UK Company
Carmelite House, 50 Victoria Embankment
London EC4Y 0DZ

Impression number    5
Year                 2017

Cover illustration by Peter Lubach
Illustrations by Planman Technologies
Typeset in ITC Stone Serif Medium 10/12.5 by Planman Technologies
Printed in Great Britain by CPI Group (UK) Ltd, Croydon, CR0 4YY

A catalogue record for this title is available from the British Library.

ISBN: 978 1444 177060

# Contents

# Introduction

## About the series

*Ready to Go Lessons* is a series of photocopiable resource books providing creative teaching strategies for primary teachers. These books support the revised Cambridge Primary curriculum frameworks for English, Mathematics and Science at Stages 1–6 (ages 5–11). They have been written by experienced primary teachers to reflect the different teaching approaches recommended in the Cambridge Primary Teacher Guides. The books contain lesson plans and photocopiable support materials, with a wide range of activities and appropriate ideas for assessment and differentiation. As the books are intended for international schools we have taken care to ensure that they are culturally sensitive.

## Cambridge Primary

The Cambridge Primary curriculum frameworks show schools how to develop the learners' knowledge, skills and understanding in English, Mathematics and Science. They provide a secure foundation in preparation for the Cambridge Secondary 1 (lower secondary) curriculum. The ideas in this book can also be easily incorporated into existing curriculum frameworks already in your school.

## How to use this book

This book covers each of the units of the scheme of work for English at Stage 3. It can be worked through systematically, or used to support areas where you feel you need more ideas. It is not prescriptive – it gives ideas and suggestions for you to incorporate into your own planning and teaching as you see fit.

Each step-by-step lesson plan shows you the learning objectives you will cover, the resources you will need and how to deliver the lesson. The lesson plans offer recommendations for suitable texts in the 'Resources' section, however the plans and photocopiable pages have been designed to be as flexible as possible so that if you don't have the specific text the lesson plan and photocopiable page can usually easily be adapted to use an alternative. Each lesson includes a Starter activity, Main activities and a Plenary that draws the lesson to a close and recaps the learning objectives. Success criteria are provided in the form of questions to help you assess the learners' level of understanding. The 'Differentiation' section provides support for the less-able learners and extension ideas for the more able.

For each lesson plan there is at least one supporting photocopiable activity page. At the end of each unit there are also suggestions for assessment activities. Answers to activities can be found at www.hoddereducation.com/cambridgeextras.

## Learning objectives

The *English Curriculum Framework* provides a set of learning objectives for each stage. At the start of each lesson you need to re-phrase the learning objectives into child-friendly language so that you can share them with the learners at the outset. It sometimes helps to express them as *We are learning to / about …* statements or an enquiry question. This really does help the learners to focus on the lesson's outcomes. For example: 'Use reading as a model for writing dialogue' (Stage 3) could be introduced to the learners at the start of the lesson as: *We are learning to write direct speech.* To avoid unnecessary repetition we have not included such statements at the start of each lesson plan but it is understood that the teacher would do this.

The speaking and listening objectives have been creatively threaded through the units in order to actively engage the learners with the text type, supporting the *Talk for Writing* approaches. Similarly the grammar and punctuation objectives and skills have been linked into the reading and writing activities in order to contextualise the learning more fully.

## Objective coverage

The overview chart on pages 6–7 shows you how the learning objectives are covered in the lessons in this book. You will notice that although the schemes of work include objectives for phonics, spelling and handwriting these have generally not been included in the books. *Letters and Sounds* suggests that good practice would be to teach a separate phonics, spelling and handwriting lesson. For that reason these books focus mainly on the vocabulary, grammar and punctuation, reading, writing, speaking and listening objectives. The phonics, spelling and handwriting objectives not covered in this book are: 3PSV1, 3PSV2, 3PSV3, 3PSV4, 3Wp1, 3Wp2 and 3Wp3.

## Success criteria

These are the measures that the teacher and, eventually, the learner will be able to use to assess the outcome of the learning that has taken place in each lesson. They are included as a series of questions, which will help you as teacher to assess the learners' understanding of the skills and knowledge covered in the lesson.

## Formative assessment

Formative assessment is on-going assessment that occurs in every lesson and informs the teacher and learners of the progress they are making, linked to the success criteria. The types of questions to ask that will support teachers in making formative assessments have been incorporated into each lesson in the 'Success criteria' sections.

One of the advantages of formative assessment is that any problems that arise during the lesson can be responded to immediately. Formative assessment influences the next steps in learning and may influence changes in planning and / or delivery for subsequent lessons.

## Summative assessment

Summative assessment is essential at the end of each unit of work to assess exactly what the learners know, understand and can do. The assessment sections at the end of each unit are designed to provide you with a variety of opportunities to check the learners' understanding of the unit. These activities can include specific questions for teachers to ask, activities for the learners to carry out (independently, in pairs or in groups) or written assessment.

The information gained from both the formative and summative assessment ideas can then be used to inform future planning in order to close any gaps in the learners' understanding as recommended by *Assessment for Learning* (AFL).

## Appropriate use of ICT

At the planning stage teachers need to consider how the use of ICT in a lesson will enhance the learning process. Ensure that the ICT resources you use support and promote the learners' understanding of the learning objectives. Activities included in this book have been designed to be carried out without the need for state-of-the-art ICT facilities. Suggestions have also been included for schools with internet access and / or the use of interactive whiteboards. This is in order to cater for most teachers' needs.

In these lessons the author sometimes asks for the teacher to display an enlarged version of the photocopiable page at the front of the class. We have not specified whether this should be using an overhead projector, interactive whiteboard or flipchart, as schools will have different resources available to them.

We hope that using these resources will give you confidence and creative ideas in delivering the Cambridge Primary curriculum framework.

**Emily Budinger, Series Editor**

# Overview chart

## Elements of a story

### Learning objectives

- Identify different types of stories and typical story themes. (3Rf5)
- Make a record of information drawn from a text, e.g. by completing a chart. (3Wn4)
- Begin to infer meanings beyond the literal, e.g. about motives and character. (3Rf4)

### Resources

*The Diary of a Killer Cat* by Anne Fine (Puffin); a large selection of familiar picture books and stories around the theme of home and family; photocopiable page 9.

### Starter

- Introduce *The Diary of a Killer Cat* by Anne Fine. From the title, what do the learners think the book might be about?
- Read the book aloud to the learners. This will take about 20 minutes. Do not let the learners see the illustrations for now. As you read, ask the learners:
  - *What do you think Tuffy looks like?*
  - *What picture do you have in your head at this point?*
  - *How do you feel about Tuffy? Has this changed?*
  - *What do you predict will happen next?*
  - *Can you imagine what Thumper looks like? Can you 'see' him?*

### Main activities

- Discuss with the learners how it is important to be able to express feelings and likes and dislikes about what they read.
- Distribute photocopiable page 9 and display an enlarged version.
- Check the learners understand the table, and model how to complete it using their ideas about *The Diary of a Killer Cat*.
- Ask the learners to work in pairs to complete the first empty column of the table, discussing their ideas before writing them down, then to discuss the two points at the bottom of the page.

- Next, ask the learners to choose two or three stories from a selection of familiar picture books or longer stories on the theme of home and family. Ask them to to fill in the table for these stories, again discussing their ideas first.
- As the learners practise this skill, they will become more confident in extracting basic information from new texts.

### Plenary

- Ask the learners to 'hot seat' the main characters of Tuffy and Ellie in small groups. Ask: *How did you feel when you found the rabbit?*
- Tell the learners that Anne Fine's books often have a family theme and often explore the idea that appearances can be deceptive.

### Success criteria

Ask the learners:

- Who are the main characters in *The Diary of a Killer Cat*?
- What is a setting?
- What was good or well written in the story?
- Why is it that we like the 'killer' cat even though he is a 'baddie' in this story?
- What does Tuffy think of Ellie's dad?

### Ideas for differentiation

**Support:** Ask these learners to pick out key words that describe one of the characters from *The Diary of a Killer Cat*, and then to draw the character, capturing these elements.

**Extension:** Ask these learners to work together in a group, taking turns to persuade the other members of the group to read a particular book, providing three reasons for reading it.

Name: _____

# The parts of a story

1.   Complete the table below for some books you have read.

| | | | |
|---|---|---|---|
| Name of book | | | |
| Main character | | | |
| Setting | | | |
| Plot | | | |
| Theme | | | |
| Favourite part of the story | | | |
| What would you change in the story? | | | |

2.   With a partner, discuss why each of these statements could be true, then write down your ideas.

| | |
|---|---|
| Tuffy is a bad cat. | |
| Tuffy is a hero. | |

# Revisiting prefixes

● Extend earlier work on prefixes and suffixes. (3PSV6)

● Use a dictionary or electronic means to find the spelling and meaning of words. (3PSV8)

● Organise words or information alphabetically using first two letters. (3PSV9)

**Resources**

Photocopiable page 11; a range of dictionaries.

## Starter

- Distribute dictionaries to the learners in pairs.
- Challenge the learners to quickly look up a familiar word, for example 'tree', 'lion', 'baby', and so on.
- Ask the learners how they used the dictionary – what strategies they used.
- Ask: *What is the quickest way to find a word? What can we use to help us?* Elicit that dictionaries list words in alphabetical order.
- Discuss with the learners that knowing the alphabet and the order in which the letters come significantly speeds up finding words in a dictionary.
- Give the learners a new word to find, but this time spell the word out slowly. Repeat a few more times with different words to give the learners practice. Include words that start with the same letter so that the learners have to order using the first two letters.

## Main activities

- Remind the learners of the terms 'prefix' and 'suffix'.
- Clarify the learners' understanding. Ask: *Which goes at the beginning of a word?*
- Discuss and demonstrate how a root word can be changed using a prefix, for example 'happy' becomes 'unhappy'.
- Ask the learners in pairs and without using dictionaries to come up with a list of prefixes that they know, for example 'dis-', 're-', 'de-', 'un-', and so on.

- Ask: *How do we know which prefix to use?* How do we know whether to say 'refit' or 'unfit' – two different prefixes with two different meanings?
- Agree that we need to say the word out loud and see if it sounds right or check in a dictionary or thesaurus.
- Ask the learners to work in pairs to complete photocopiable page 11, using dictionaries to help them.

## Plenary

- Using the prefixes collected during the Main activity, create a table of prefixes on a large piece of paper for future reference and class display.
- Ask the learners to share the words they have found with their partner and use the words to annotate the class list.
- Discuss any new vocabulary and model looking up unfamiliar words in a dictionary.

**Success criteria**

Ask the learners:

● What is a prefix?

● Explain how a prefix changes a root word.

● How do we know which prefix is the right one to use?

● Do all prefixes have root words? Can you think of any that are an exception?

**Ideas for differentiation**

**Support:** Provide these learners with an alphabet strip, differentiated dictionaries and adult support during the Main activity.

**Extension:** Ask these learners to use a dictionary to find other words with the prefixes 'de-', 're-' and pre-' and write them in a sentence.

Name: _____

unsure

# Prefixes

Use a dictionary to help you with these questions.

1.  Complete this sentence:

    Prefixes go at the _____ of a word.

2.  Change the meaning of these words by adding the prefix 'un-' or 'dis-' to each one:

    a)  _____fit      b)  _____do      c)  _____appear

    d)  _____true      e)  _____fair      f)  _____happy

3.  Find two more words that start with:

    a)  un- _____      un- _____

    b)  dis- _____      dis- _____

4.  Add the prefix 're-' to these words and find their new meaning:

| Root word | Add 're-' | New meaning |
|-----------|-----------|-------------|
| build     |           |             |
| arrange   |           |             |
| tell      |           |             |

5.  Find the meaning for any **three** of these words:

    depart      defrost      depend      despair

    deduct      defuse      deflate      destroy

    a)  Word: _____ Meaning: _____

    b)  Word: _____ Meaning: _____

    c)  Word: _____ Meaning: _____

6.  Find two words that have the prefix 'pre-':

    a)  _____      b)  _____

# Creating a character profile

## Learning objectives

- Write portraits of characters. (3Wf3)
- Begin to infer meanings beyond the literal, e.g. about motives and character. (3Rf4)
- Consider how choice of words can heighten meaning. (3PSV11)

## Resources

Copies of a range of books that the learners are familiar with, one for each learner, including *The Diary of a Killer Cat* by Anne Fine (Puffin) if the learners know it; paper for three signs; photocopiable pages 13 and 14; scissors.

## Starter

- Display three signs: 'Looks', 'Behaviour' and 'Feelings', around the classroom.
- Create word cards from photocopiable page 13 and distribute one card to each learner. Ask them to decide which characteristic their word describes and stand by the appropriate sign.
- Ask the groups by each sign to share their words and agree that they are all in the right place. Collect in the cards and repeat the activity.

## Main activities

- Ask the learners to describe themselves to the person sitting next to them. Ask some of the learners to share their descriptions with the rest of the class. (The learners will tend to focus on physical appearance.)
- Discuss how characters can be described in terms of how they look and behave, and the feelings they express. Discuss how writers find ways to 'show' the reader this information rather than just telling them.
- Display an enlarged version of photocopiable page 14 and use it to capture characteristics of Ellie from *The Diary of a Killer Cat*. The learners haven't seen a picture of her so hopefully they will focus on feelings and behaviours. (Use a character from another book if you don't have this book.)

- Distribute photocopiable page 14 to each learner, make the range of familiar books available and ask the learners to fill in the photocopiable page for a character that they are very familiar with, either from *The Diary of a Killer Cat* (for example Tuffy) or from another book that they have a copy of.
- Ask the learners to look through the book to collect descriptions under each heading then use the vocabulary to write a character profile.
- As they are carrying out the task ask: *How do you know? Where is the evidence in the text?*

## Plenary

- Read out a few descriptions the learners have written. Can the rest of the class recognise the character?
- Put the cards from the Starter in a bag and ask the learners to take turns to take a card, read it and then try to think of a character they know who has that characteristic.

## Success criteria

Ask the learners:

- How do we know the 'killer cat' is clever?
- How does Anne Fine 'show' us that?
- Give three words that describe the appearance, behaviour and feelings of a character.
- How do writers build a picture of their characters?

## Ideas for differentiation

**Support:** Ask these learners to draw their chosen character then write the description in a list style.

**Extension:** Ask these learners to try to draw each other's character based only on the information in the descriptions.

# Characteristics

| | | |
|---|---|---|
| brown eyes | sly | lonely |
| pointed nose | selfish | shy |
| curly hair | childish | nervous |
| tall | boisterous | confident |
| dressed smartly | loud | grumpy |
| wearing a hat | caring | excited |
| elegant | bossy | relaxed |
| scruffy | easy going | jealous |
| smiling | lazy | happy |

Name: _____

# Describing a character

1. Collect descriptions about a character under these headings:

| Looks | Behaviour | Feelings |
|---|---|---|
| | | |
| | | |
| | | |
| | | |
| | | |
| | | |
| | | |
| | | |
| | | |
| | | |
| | | |
| | | |
| | | |

2. Now use your descriptions to write a character profile.

*Cambridge Primary: Ready to Go Lessons for English Stage 3* © Hodder & Stoughton Ltd 2013

# Direct speech

**Learning objectives**

- Explore vocabulary for introducing and concluding dialogue, e.g. said, asked. (3PSV13)
- Use reading as a model for writing dialogue. (3Wf8)
- Consider words that make an impact, e.g. adjectives and powerful verbs. (3Rf7)

**Resources**

A variety of picture books, set in a familiar setting, with plenty of direct speech; photocopiable page 16; scissors.

## Starter

- Distribute the picture books one between two learners, and ask the learners to find examples of how the writer has shown when a character is speaking. Ask: *How can you tell what is being said?*
- Discuss the terms 'dialogue' and 'direct speech' and elicit from the learners that they refer to the words in a text that are spoken / said.
- Using the ideas from the learners, compile a list of rules for direct speech, for example: 'Use speech marks to show which part is being said.', 'The punctuation goes inside the speech marks.', 'Start a new line for each new person speaking.', 'State who is talking, unless it is obvious.'

## Main activities

- Distribute photocopiable page 16 and ask the learners to work individually to correctly punctuate the sentences at the top of the page.
- Ask the learners in pairs to look again at their picture book and collect three different ways of saying **said**, for example 'begged', 'asked', and so on.
- Ask the learners in pairs to cut out the set of words from one of their photocopiable pages and place them face down in front of them.

- Ask the pairs to take turns to turn over one of the cards and use the new word to replace 'said' in the sentences at the top of the page. Encourage the learners to try out a few and see which is best.
- Ask them to discuss how the meaning changes in each case.
- Ask them to cross out 'said' in each of the sentences on photocopiable page 16 and replace it with a word of their choice.
- Share the different choices the learners have made with the rest of the class, reading the sentences aloud to emphasise the differences.

## Plenary

- Write the following sentence on the board: 'Come in out of the rain said John.'
- Ask: *How can we make this dialogue better? Can we change the meaning by choosing a different word for 'said'?*
- Provide a display area and explain that the learners will collect powerful alternatives to 'said' for display.

**Success criteria**

Ask the learners:

- What is dialogue?
- Why do writers use direct speech?
- Why do we try to find more exciting words to use than 'said'?
- What word for 'said' could you use if somebody was angry?

**Ideas for differentiation**

**Support:** Ask these learners to read and act out the sentences to see which word for 'said' is best. Provide adult support.

**Extension:** Ask these learners to use a thesaurus to find alternative words for 'said'.

# Using direct speech

1. Add the missing speech marks.

   a) Look over there said David.

   b) Why can't I help said the small boy.

   c) Someone spilt the milk said her mother.

   d) It's dark outside she said.

   e) Hurry up we're late said Kate.

2. Look at these alternatives to the word 'said'. With a partner, see what happens when you replace 'said' in the sentences above with one of these words.

✂

| laughed | pleaded | grumbled |
|---|---|---|
| cried | yelled | mumbled |
| ordered | replied | questioned |
| shouted | screamed | suggested |
| begged | answered | argued |
| giggled | sang | whispered |

*Cambridge Primary: Ready to Go Lessons for English Stage 3* © Hodder & Stoughton Ltd 2013

# Paragraphs

## Learning objectives

- Plan main points as a structure for story writing. (3Wf5)
- Sustain the reading of 48 and 64 page books, noting how a text is organised into sections or chapters. (3Rf1)
- Speak clearly and confidently in a range of contexts, including longer speaking turns. (3SL1)

## Resources

Photocopiable page 18; glue, scissors, large pieces of paper.

## Starter

- Distribute photocopiable page 18 and ask the learners to work in pairs.
- Ask them to cut out and order the pictures, discussing their choices.
- Provide the learners with large pieces of paper and ask them to stick the title square in the middle of the bottom of the piece of paper and organise the pictures in a hill shape over it.

## Main activities

- Ask: *Why do writers use paragraphs?* Briefly discuss the learners' answers and clarify that a new paragraph can indicate a:
  - change in time or setting
  - change in the focus or character
  - change of direction or action
  - new speaker in dialogue.

- Discuss how in a retelling of *The Diary of a Killer Cat*, each picture could be a new paragraph.
- Ask the learners in pairs to write notes next to each picture on the details of plot, character, setting or dialogue that might go in each paragraph. Model writing notes for the first picture.
- Ask the learners to check accuracy by retelling the story within their pairs.

## Plenary

- Pick five pairs of learners to use their notes about one picture to tell one section or paragraph of the story to the rest of the class.
- Discuss how the structure makes the story easier to follow.

## Success criteria

Ask the learners:

- How does a writer show a new paragraph?
- What is a story structure? How can we use it?
- What would happen if a section was missed out?
- Can you give three examples of settings in a story you know?

## Ideas for differentiation

**Support:** Ask these learners to add pictures and words to their plan.

**Extension:** Ask these learners to consider how to open and close paragraphs for the best effect.

# Using paragraphs

## The Diary of a Killer Cat
## by
## Anne Fine

# Describing settings using our senses

## Learning objectives

- Develop descriptions of settings in stories. (3Wf2)
- Consider words that make an impact, e.g. adjectives and powerful verbs. (3Rf7)
- Consider how choice of words can heighten meaning. (3PSV11)

## Resources

Photographs of places familiar to the learners; dice; photocopiable pages 20 and 21.

## Starter

- Display a large version of the table on photocopiable page 20 and write the following key on the board:
  1 = see
  2 = hear
  3 = touch or feel
  4 = smell
  5 = see and touch
  6 = hear and smell.
- Select a photograph of a familiar place and conceal it from the learners.
- Ask them to take turns to roll the dice to collect clues using the key, for example if they roll a 2 tell them something you can hear in the place, using interesting vocabulary.
- Write the clues in the correct sections of your enlarged table.
- Continue until the learners are able to guess the place.
- Provide the learners in small groups with a few photographs of familiar places and a dice then ask them to play the game, taking turns to do the describing. Remind them to use interesting vocabulary.

## Main activities

- Repeat the game with one learner describing the picture as another rolls the dice, whilst the rest of the class watch. Turn what the learner says into a description by linking the ideas together, for example:

- 'I can see a beach with grass at the edge.' – *He walked over the grassy sand dunes and saw a beautiful golden sandy beach.*
- 'There is nothing else in the picture.' – *He was all alone as there was nothing but golden sand as far as the eye could see.*
- 'I can feel the wind on my face.' – *As he walked from the shelter of the grassy sand dunes he felt a fresh breeze coming from across the sea.*
- Distribute photocopiable page 21 to the learners to use as a writing frame to plan and write a description of a familiar setting of their choosing. Remind them to use the best vocabulary they can.

## Plenary

- Ask the learners to listen to each other's descriptions and check they have used the senses.
- Ask: *Can you see a picture in your mind of your partner's setting from their description?*
- Ask: *What have we read recently with a vivid description?*

## Success criteria

Ask the learners:

- Which of our senses gives us the most information about a setting?
- Why are descriptions using more than one of the senses better?
- How can your vocabulary choices help with describing settings?
- Why is it easier to create descriptions with exciting vocabulary about settings you know well?

## Ideas for differentiation

**Support:** Ask these learners to work in a small adult-helper led group and use the photographs from the Starter, collecting descriptions on photocopiable page 20.

**Extension:** Ask these learners to look in recently read texts for examples of good descriptions of settings and to look at how the writer used the senses.

Name: _____

# Describing using senses

1.  Write some notes in the boxes below about a place you know well.
    Write what you can see, smell, hear and feel.

2.  Use your ideas to write a description of a setting.

*Cambridge Primary: Ready to Go Lessons for English Stage 3* © Hodder & Stoughton Ltd 2013

Name: _____

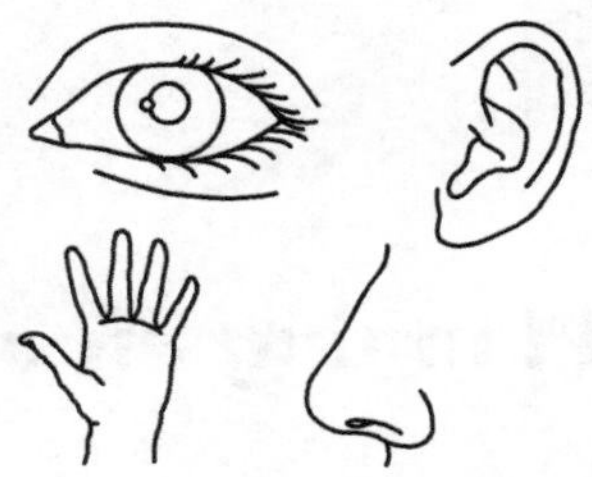

# Describing using senses

1.  Use this table to collect ideas for writing a description.

| What can you see? | • _____ |
| | • _____ |
| | • _____ |
| | • _____ |
| What can you hear? | • _____ |
| | • _____ |
| | • _____ |
| What can you feel or touch? | • _____ |
| | • _____ |
| What can you smell? | • _____ |

2.  Use your ideas to write a description of a setting.

_____

_____

_____

_____

_____

_____

_____

_____

# Planning an oral story

## Learning objectives

- Plan main points as a structure for story writing. (3Wf5)
- Begin to organise writing in sections or paragraphs in extended stories. (3Wf6)
- Adapt tone of voice, use of vocabulary and non-verbal features for different audiences. (3SL2)

## Resources

Photocopiable pages 18 and 23.

## Starter

- Display an enlarged copy of photocopiable page 23.
- Divide the class into five groups and give each a heading from one of the boxes. Using the plot of *The Diary of a Killer Cat*, or another book that the learners are very familiar with, ask each group to prepare a brief explanation of the events in their given part of the story. Display the pictures from photocopiable page 18 to help.
- When all the groups are ready, ask the learners to tell the story orally, going round each group in turn so that the whole class speaks.
- As the story unfolds, write words and phrases in each box on the enlarged copy of photocopiable page 23.

## Main activities

- Tell the learners that they are going to plan their own versions of *The Diary of a Killer Cat* or the book you have been using in this unit, in preparation for telling it orally. Allow them to change as little or as much of the story as appropriate for their level.
- Distribute individual copies of photocopiable page 23 and ask the learners to make notes in each box about their version of the story. Point out the notes you made on the enlarged photocopiable page and encourage them to make similar notes.

- Encourage them to stop after they have finished each box and practise telling their story so far to check they have enough detail and it is starting to make sense.

## Plenary

- Give the learners an opportunity to practise their story-telling skills in groups. Remind them to be supportive about each other's stories and not to interrupt. All the stories will be slightly different.
- Tell the learners that next time they will use their plans to write their story, using each section as a new paragraph.

## Success criteria

Ask the learners:

- Does your plan have enough detail for you to tell the story?
- Why is it useful to tell the story before starting to write it?
- How do you think the heading sections will help organise the writing next time?
- How can you use your voice to draw in the listener?

## Ideas for differentiation

**Support:** In the Starter activity, allocate these learners the beginning of the story only. In the Main activity ask them to produce a collaborative plan and encourage them to use role-play to act out ideas.

**Extension:** Ask these learners to begin to consider vocabulary choices that are going to excite and interest the reader.

Name: _____

# Planning a story

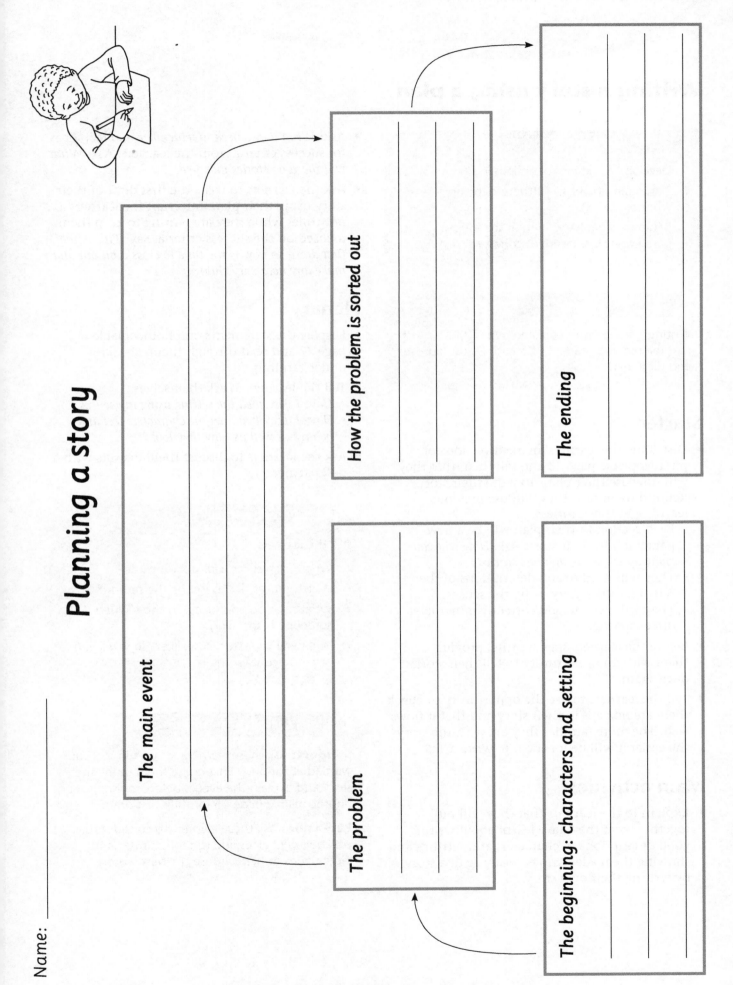

**The main event**

**How the problem is sorted out**

**The ending**

**The problem**

**The beginning: characters and setting**

# Writing a story using a plan

## Learning objectives

- Develop descriptions of settings in stories. (3Wf2)
- Plan main points as a structure for story writing. (3Wf5)
- Begin to organise writing in sections or paragraphs in extended stories. (3Wf6)

## Resources

Writing books; photocopiable pages 23 (completed and marked), 25 and 27; thesauruses and dictionaries.

## Starter

- Distribute the learners' marked versions of photocopiable page 23 and tell them that they will now use their plans to write their story. Remind them how they will use previous learning in their stories:
  - Each section in their plan will be a new paragraph in their story. Ask: *How will you show a new paragraph has started?*
  - They will need to add descriptions of the settings in the story using the senses.
  - They will need to add correctly punctuated direct speech.
- Before the learners start writing, provide them with an opportunity to tell their stories once again.
- Tell the learners to use the opportunity to check there are no gaps in their story and that it flows well. The more familiar they are with the story the easier it will be for them to write it.

## Main activities

- Explain to the learners that they will pull together what they have learnt about writing good descriptions of characters and settings and showing the reader who is speaking in a story by writing their own story.

- Ask: *What do we need to remember?* Collect ideas for success criteria from the learners. Ask: *What will the good stories look like?*
- Ask the learners to write the first draft of their story using their plan. Interrupt the learners a few times while they are writing to keep them focused on the success criteria. Say: *This is the first draft, so now is the time to cross a bit out and make any necessary changes.*

## Plenary

- Display the statements on photocopiable page 27 and read through them, checking understanding.
- Tell the learners to ask themselves:
  - *Have I described the setting using my senses?*
  - *Have I described how the characters feel and behave as well as how they look?*
- Ask the learners to discuss their answers with a talk partner.

## Success criteria

Ask the learners:

- What will a successful story include?
- Which senses best describe the setting?
- What rules do you follow to show when someone is speaking?
- What will your story look like? How will you organise your writing?

## Ideas for differentiation

**Support:** Ask these learners to work in a group with adult support. Encourage them to tell the story and explain the events before writing, using photocopiable page 25 for their first draft.

**Extension:** Ask these learners to consider their vocabulary choices and use thesauruses and dictionaries to help choose the best words.

Name: _____

# Writing a story using a plan

Use this table to write the first draft of your story.

| | |
|---|---|
| **The beginning** (include descriptions of the characters and setting) | |
| **The problem** | |
| **The main event** | |
| **How the problem is sorted out** | |
| **The ending** | |

# Editing and improving writing

### Learning objectives

- Maintain accurate use of capital letters and full stops in showing sentences. (3GPw1)
- Consider how choice of words can heighten meaning. (3PSV11)
- Learn the basic conventions of speech punctuation and begin to use speech marks. (3GPw2)

### Resources

Completed first draft of story or completed photocopiable page 25; photocopiable page 27; writing books.

## Starter

- Ask the learners: *How can we make our stories better?* Allow them to reflect on what they have learnt.
- Distribute photocopiable page 27 and ensure that each learner has their draft story to hand.
- Read and discuss the checklist with the learners, discussing how they might use it to improve their story, for example changing words to add greater detail to the descriptions of the characters and settings.
- Ask the learners to remind each other of the rules for direct speech. Ask: *Have you kept to the rules?*

## Main activities

- Ask the learners to use their checklist to make notes around their first draft, circling areas that need to be improved in the final version. Tell them to bear in mind that their partner will mark their story against the success criteria. Ask: *How will you show a new paragraph has started?*
- Tell the learners to write their final version of the story.
- When they think they have a final version, ask them to read it through at least twice in a mumbled voice, listening to what they are reading and checking it makes sense.

- When they're happy with their final version, ask them to start checking off the success criteria on photocopiable page 27, adding examples of words they have used.
- Ask them to swap stories with their partner, and ask their partner to read their story and fill in the second column on the table.

## Plenary

- Discuss giving feedback to each other and introduce the criteria of two stars and a wish: a learner should say two things that are good about the story and one thing that could be improved.
- Model an example using one of the learner's stories:
  - Star: I liked the way you explained how Tuffy was innocent.
  - Star: You accurately used speech marks to show when someone is speaking.
  - Wish: Try to use other words for 'said' and 'asked'.

### Success criteria

Ask the learners:

- Have you written a successful story?
- How do you know?
- How have you shown what the characters are saying?
- Which words for 'said' have you used?
- What sort of additions or changes did you make after checking the success criteria?

### Ideas for differentiation

**Support:** Ask these learners to work through the success criteria as a group, then design an illustration to go with each paragraph.

**Extension:** Ask these learners to consider how to link the events in each paragraph.

Name: _____

# The author's checklist

There is a lot to remember when writing a story.

Use this checklist to help you.

| Success criteria | Author | Partner |
|---|---|---|
| I have read my story aloud at least twice to check it makes sense. | | |
| I have used full stops and capital letters to show the start and end of sentences. | | |
| I have chosen these interesting and powerful words to describe the characters: | | |
| I have described the setting using my senses. | | |
| I have used my plan to put the story into five paragraphs. | | |
| I have used some direct speech to show when the characters are speaking. | | |
| I have used these words instead of 'said': | | |

# Unit assessment

- What is a setting?
- How do writers describe a setting? What do they use to help them?
- If you were writing a story with a familiar setting where would it be?

- What are the different sections you would use to write a good story?
- What is dialogue / direct speech?
- How do we change our voice when we read dialogue?

## Summative assessment activities

Observe the learners while they play these games. You will quickly be able to identify those who appear to be confident and those who may need additional support.

### Spot the genre

This game helps the learners to identify story settings in a variety of texts.

**You will need:**

A variety of short stories and picture books; a piece of A4 paper for each group divided in half with two headings: 'Setting' and 'Evidence'.

**What to do**

- Divide the learners into teams of four or five. Give the same number of books to each group (four or five books is sufficient).

- Ask each group to nominate one reader and one writer for each book. The reader should pick up a story and start reading out loud. The rest of the group must listen. When they hear a setting they should tell the writer to write it down and to copy the phrase from the text into the evidence column.

- The pace could be increased with a time limit, if appropriate.

- The winning group is the first to identify and provide evidence for six settings (there will be more than one setting in most of the stories).

### Describe the settings

This game gives the learners an opportunity to play with words and descriptions.

**You will need:**

A list containing a variety of settings that the learners could be familiar with, for example their garden, a car, a beach, a forest or wood, a play park.

**What to do**

- Provide the learners in pairs with the list.
- Ask them to work in pairs to create a sentence, for example: First one learner may say 'the woods'; their partner could say 'the dark woods'; the first learner could add 'on the edge of the dark woods'; and so on until a vivid description is created.
- The learners should write down the final sentence, then pick another setting and repeat.

Distribute photocopiable page 29. Read through the questions with the learners to check understanding before letting them complete the page. They should work independently.

Name: _____

# Stories with familiar settings

1. Look at the sentences below and see if you can add information to them. The first one has been done for you.

   a) Tuffy sat on the rug.

      Feeling very proud of himself, Tuffy stretched out his legs then sat comfortably on the fluffy rug and admired his catch.

   b) Tuffy watched Dad.

      _____

      _____.

   c) Tuffy felt sad.

      _____

      _____.

2. Write an example of how a writer shows direct speech.

   _____

3. What rules do we have to follow for direct speech?

   - _____

   - _____

   - _____

   - _____

4. Think of your school's playground. Write a description of it using as many senses as you can. Think about what you can: see, hear, smell, taste and touch.

   _____

   _____

   _____

   _____

# Identifying instructions

## Learning objectives

- Understand and use the terms 'fact', 'fiction' and 'non-fiction'. (3Rf8)
- Locate information in non-fiction texts using contents page and index. (3Rn2)
- Consider ways that information is set out on page and on screen, e.g. lists, charts, bullet points. (3Rn4)

## Resources

Photocopiable pages 31 and 32; a range of instructional texts, e.g. *Mud Pies and Other Recipes* by Marjorie Winslow (Walker Books), *Revolting Recipes* by Roald Dahl (Red Fox), 'how to' books, craft books and recipe books; coloured pencils or highlighters; *George's Marvellous Medicine* by Roald Dahl (Puffin).

## Starter

- Display an enlarged version of photocopiable page 31 and distribute copies to the learners.
- Read the texts together, then give the learners an opportunity to look at them for a minute and discuss them with a partner. Ask:
  - *Are these texts fiction or non-fiction? How can you tell?*
  - *Where do we find these types of text?*
  - *What type of text are they? Why have they been written?*
  - *Which features make them instructions?*
  - *Are they all instructions? Why do they look different?*

## Main activities

- Display an enlarged version of photocopiable page 32. Together with the learners, fill in the table for each of the instructions on photocopiable page 31.
- Discuss the quality of the instructions. Ask:
  - *Are they fit for purpose?*
  - *Could you use them?*
  - *If not, what is wrong with them? How can they be improved?*

- Make a large range of instructions available and distribute photocopiable page 32 to each learner. Ask them to work in pairs to find four different sets of instructions (as different as possible – for example not all recipes, or they will have little to compare) and use the table to collect the features of them.
- Explain to the learners that not all of the instructions will have all of the features in the table.
- When they've finished, ask them to discuss the quality of their four sets of instructions. Did it matter when a set of instructions didn't have all of the listed features?

## Plenary

- Ask some of the pairs of learners to share with the rest of the class what they have found.
- Discuss the minimum features required for a good set of instructions.
- Discuss the other features that the learners found: safety advice, warnings, alternative options or ingredients, and so on.

## Success criteria

Ask the learners:

- What is the difference between fiction and non-fiction?
- How can we identify instructions? What features should we find?
- Which features are the most important in instructions? (Order of instructions? Bullet points?) Why?
- What similarities and differences have you seen in the instructions we have read today?

## Ideas for differentiation

**Support:** Ask these learners to use coloured pencils or highlighters to mark the features directly on to photocopiable page 31.

**Extension:** Provide these learners with fiction texts with (non-fiction) instructions in, such as *George's Marvellous Medicine* by Roald Dahl (Puffin) and ask: *Where does this fit in?* (It is a mixture of fiction and non-fiction.)

# Identifying instructions

## Grilled cheese on toast

This recipe will serve one person; you can double it if you are extra hungry!

**You will need:**

- Two slices of bread
- Butter
- Grated cheese of your choice

1. First pre-heat the grill to high.
2. Toast the bread on one side only.
3. Remove the bread from the grill and spread butter on the untoasted side.
4. Sprinkle the cheese on top.
5. Place back under the grill until the cheese has melted.
6. Remove and place on a plate ready to eat.

Don't forget to turn off the grill!

How to clean your teeth. You will need: a toothbrush, some toothpaste and water. Firstly pick up your toothbrush. Dip the toothbrush in the water to make it wet. Put a small amount of toothpaste on the brush. Begin brushing your teeth until they are clean. Finally rinse your toothbrush and mouth with water.

## How to cross the road safely

1. Look for a safe place where you can see both ways.
2. Stand on the pavement a safe distance from the kerb.
3. Look both ways to check if anything is coming.
4. When it is clear and safe both ways, cross quickly and carefully.

Name: _____

# Finding information
# in instructions

Use this table to collect information about four different sets of instructions.

| | | | | |
|---|---|---|---|---|
| Type of instructions: | | | | |
| Title or aim: | | | | |
| Includes a 'you will need' list? | | | | |
| Includes pictures or diagrams? | | | | |
| Is written in the order you have to do the tasks? | | | | |
| Includes numbered or bullet points? | | | | |
| Is in an easy-to-read layout, in sections? | | | | |
| Consists of short, simple sentences? | | | | |
| Any other interesting elements: | | | | |

*Cambridge Primary: Ready to Go Lessons for English Stage 3* © Hodder & Stoughton Ltd 2013

# Rules for instructions

- Identify the main purpose of a text. (3Rn6)
- Consider ways that information is set out on page and on screen, e.g. lists, charts, bullet points. (3Rn4)
- Take turns in discussion, building on what others have said. (3SL3)

**Resources**

Photocopiable pages 34 and 35; scissors; A4 paper and glue.

## Starter

- Explain to the learners that they are going to come up with a set of rules for good instructions. Ask: *What features should I find in a good set of instructions?*
- Ask the learners to work in groups of four to six to collect as many ideas as they can.
- After a few minutes, collect one idea at a time from each group and write it up on the board. As a class, decide which features are the most important and create a list.
- This list will be referred to throughout the unit; ensure the following are included on it:
  - title or aim of the instructions
  - what you need
  - written instructions (with some pictures or diagrams)
  - a series of actions presented in the right order as numbered or bulleted points
  - clear, easy-to-follow language.

## Main activities

- Distribute photocopiable page 34 to each learner and begin to read it out loud, continuing until someone notices that the instructions are not in the correct order. If necessary, make the strange order more explicit by acting puzzled and questioning the instructions.
- Agree with the learners that these instructions are a bit confusing and need sorting out. Ask: *Where should we start?* Agree that you should start with the title / aim.

- Ask the learners to cut the instructions into strips as indicated and to organise the instructions into the correct order, first locating the title / aim.
- Ask the learners to glue down the instructions in the correct order on a new piece of paper, leaving room for diagrams and illustrations.
- Encourage the learners to illustrate the instructions with pictures and diagrams to make them as attractive and easy to follow as possible.

## Plenary

- Using an example from one of the learners, ask:
  - *Without reading, how can you tell these are instructions?* (Presentation and layout.)
  - *What features can you see?* (Refer to the rules from the Starter activity.)
  - *Are these instructions good? Could we use them?* (Note that the recipe has no quantities for the ingredients. Is that a problem?)

**Success criteria**

Ask the learners:

- What are the rules for writing instructions?
- Why do we use numbering or bullet points?
- Does there have to be a diagram in a set of instructions?
- What happens if the rules for writing good instructions are not followed?

**Ideas for differentiation**

**Support:** Provide these learners with photocopiable page 35 to reorder, instead of page 34.

**Extension:** Ask these learners to consider the presentation of a recipe and create a poster-style recipe, using the recipe on photocopiable page 34 but rewriting it and including pictures and diagrams.

# Mixed-up instructions: Making cupcakes

Cut out the instructions below and stick them onto a separate piece of paper. Add some diagrams or pictures to make the instructions attractive and easy to follow.

Eat and enjoy!

Beat the butter and sugar together until light and fluffy.

Spoon the mixture into paper cases and put in the oven for 15–20 minutes.

**How to make chocolate chip cupcakes**

Add the egg to the butter and sugar.

Fold in one spoonful of flour at a time to the mixture.

Stir in the chocolate chips.

First, pre-heat the oven to 180 degrees.

Take them out of the oven and allow to cool.

You will need:

butter, sugar, flour, a lightly beaten egg, chocolate chips, muffin tin and paper cases.

 *Cambridge Primary: Ready to Go Lessons for English Stage 3* © Hodder & Stoughton Ltd 2013

# Mixed-up instructions: Making a shaker

Cut out the instructions below and stick them onto a separate piece of paper. Add some diagrams or pictures to make the instructions attractive and easy to follow.

✂ ------------------------------------------------

- Carefully put the lid on and seal it using sticky tape.

**How to make a musical shaker**

- Decorate the outside of the container with a pattern using coloured stickers, marker pens, feathers or anything else and shake it!

- Choose a container with a fitted lid.

- Pour a spoonful of dries peas or lentils into the container.

You will need: any small empty plastic container with a lid, sticky tape, a spoonful of dried peas or lentils, coloured stickers or marker pens or other art materials to decorate.

# Bossy verbs

- Extend earlier work on prefixes and suffixes. (3PSV6)
- Understand that verbs are necessary for meaning in a sentence. (3GPr5)
- Continue to improve consistency in the use of tenses. (3GPw4)

Photocopiable pages 31, 37 and 38; scissors; thesauruses.

## Starter

- Play a game of 'Prefix bingo': Display an enlarged version of the table of root words on photocopiable page 37 and distribute the bingo cards, one to each learner.
- Tell the learners to pick any six words from the displayed table and write them on their bingo card. They should write each word to the right of the line but leave the line blank for now.
- Call out one at a time the following prefixes in any order: 'un-', 'de-', 'dis-', 're-', 'pre-'. You will need to say them a few times. When the learners hear a prefix they must try to add it to the front of one of the root words on their card, writing on the line, for example if the learner has written the word 'dress' on their bingo card and you call out the prefix 'un-', they can write it in to make 'undress'.
- The winner is the first learner to correctly add a prefix to each of their words.

## Main activities

- Display an enlarged version of photocopiable page 31 and ask: *Where are the verbs here?* Underline or highlight the verbs, pointing out how they are usually at the beginning of each sentence in these texts.

- Discuss that these are called imperative or bossy verbs and are very important in instructions. Point out that in instructions the verbs are:
  - in the present tense
  - commanding the reader to do something
  - speaking straight at the reader – in the second person.
- Display the sentence: 'Fold the paper in half'. Ask the learners to identify the verb. Now change the verb to 'cut' or 'slice' to demonstrate to the learners how important it is to be correct in their choice of verb in instructions.
- Distribute photocopiable page 38 and ask the learners to carry out the activity.

## Plenary

- Ask the learners to feed back their findings. Ask: *Could any of the verbs be used in more than one of the piles?*
- Discuss how a good imperative verb can make the instructions more succinct.

Ask the learners:

- What is a prefix?
- What can you tell me about imperative or bossy verbs?
- What tense should instructions be written in?
- Give three verbs that might be used in a recipe and three verbs that could be used in a game.

**Support:** Encourage these learners to role-play the verb to help them decide which set of instructions it would be useful for.

**Extension:** Ask these learners to use thesauruses to find other examples to include in their lists.

Name: _____

# Prefix bingo

**Bingo card**

| | | |
|---|---|---|
| _____ | _____ | _____ |
| _____ | _____ | _____ |

**Root words**

| | | |
|---|---|---|
| dress | turn | mount |
| load | frost | pay |
| caution | like | pack |
| own | view | code |
| form | appear | visit |

# Bossy verbs

Cut out and sort these verbs into four piles, one for each of the following instructions:

| A playground game | A recipe | A set of directions | Instructions for making something out of paper |
|---|---|---|---|

✂ - - - - - - - - - - - - - - - - - - - - - - - - - - - - - - - - - - -

| | | | |
|---|---|---|---|
| hop | jump | move | take |
| bend | cut | cook | stretch |
| walk | run | paint | whisk |
| stir | boil | rotate | tear |
| go | spoon | skip | continue |
| fold | score | bake | face |
| add | pour | step | fry |
| turn | crouch | relax | fill |
| beat | draw | mix | colour |

*Cambridge Primary: Ready to Go Lessons for English Stage 3* © Hodder & Stoughton Ltd 2013

# Giving oral instructions

### Learning objectives

● Read and follow instructions to carry out an activity. (3Rn3)

● Listen and remember a sequence of instructions. (3SL5)

● Use ICT to write, edit and present work. (3Wp4)

### Resources

Internet access; paper and scissors; video camera; photocopiable page 40.

## Starter

• Discuss what oral instructions are. Agree that they are instructions that are spoken and they are used all the time, for example: 'Open your books and write the date.', 'Eat your dinner.'

• Allow the learners to give a few oral instructions to their partner, for example directing them around the classroom, or directing them to collect a list of items from around the classroom.

## Main activities

• Demonstrate silently, or show the learners a short film clip of someone making a paper helicopter (for example at www.youtube.com/watch?v=ujc-kdeKDfQ&feature=relmfu).

• Ask: *Could you make a paper helicopter? Could you tell someone else how to make one?*

• Play the film clip or do the demonstration again, this time giving oral instructions:
  • Take a piece of origami paper and fold it in half along the long side and then fold it again.
  • Open it out and cut along one of the fold lines, giving you a strip.
  • Fold the strip in half lengthways and then again so the two short edges meet.
  • Open out the strip and cut along one of the long fold lines.
  • Fold the other end of the strip in half lengthways, then open it out and fold a point at the end.
  • Fold the points over again to make a longer point.

• Fan out the other end by curling the strips over your finger.
• Drop from a height and watch it spin!

• Distribute pieces of paper and scissors and let the learners practise making their own paper helicopters before having a go at creating their own demonstration with commentary.

• When they've practised their demonstration, film the learners' instructions. Encourage them to introduce their demonstration, for example: 'Today I am going to show you how to make a paper helicopter.'

## Plenary

• Show the learners the film clip 'How to tie a shoelace really really fast' at www.youtube.com/watch?v=TKWL1md7Dv4.

• Ask: *What is good about these instructions?* (Fun, fast paced, ingenious, you can't believe your eyes.)

• Ask: *How could they be better?* (With the addition of some oral instructions.)

• Discuss how written instructions with a diagram or oral instructions with a demonstration are easier to follow than written or oral instructions alone.

### Success criteria

Ask the learners:

● What sort of pictures would be useful in a recipe? In a set of directions?

● Would oral instructions be useful for a recipe? Why not? (Lists of ingredients, too many stages, and so on.)

● Where would oral instruction be useful? (Short procedures, quick directions.)

### Ideas for differentiation

**Support:** Ask these learners to work together and use the writing frame on photocopiable page 40 to help collect and organise their ideas

**Extension:** Ask these learners to choose another origami item to learn to make and then write the instructions.

Name: _____

# How to make a paper helicopter

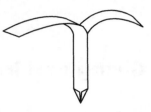

1. Use this table to help collect your ideas using words and pictures.

| You will need: | |
|---|---|
| 1. | |
| 2. | |
| 3. | |
| 4. | |
| 5. | |
| 6. | |
| 7. | |
| 8. | |

2. Use these words to help you start your sentences:

| fold | cut | then | next | curl | open | drop |
|---|---|---|---|---|---|---|

*Cambridge Primary: Ready to Go Lessons for English Stage 3* © Hodder & Stoughton Ltd 2013

# Writing instructions for games

### Learning objectives

- Establish purpose for writing, using features and style based on model texts. (3Wn2)
- Use ICT to write, edit and present work. (3Wp4)

### Resources

Photocopiable pages 38 and 42; scissors; bag or hat; digital cameras; computers.

## Starter

- Play a quick miming game using the cut-out verbs from photocopiable page 38:
  - Split the class into two or three teams.
  - Put all the action and movement verbs into a bag or hat and choose a few learners to act out the verb. The rest of the class have to guess the verb.
  - Repeat a few times to encourage some good imperative verb choices in the learners' writing.

## Main activities

- Explain to the learners that they are going to write a book of playground-game ideas to share with the rest of the school. Ask: *What games do you like to play in the playground?* Collect some of their ideas, encouraging simple games involving small groups of learners.
- Elicit from the learners which features of instructions they will need to include when they write their game instructions. Agree that they will need:
  - a title or aim of the instructions
  - a list of items needed
  - pictures or diagrams to inspire or clarify
  - to ensure that the instructions are in the right order, using numbered or bulleted points
  - to use imperative verbs to ensure clear, easy-to-follow language.
- Ask the learners to work with a partner and decide which game they are going to write instructions for. Encourage them to 'walk through' the game together, agreeing all the stages they need to include.

- Hand out photocopiable page 42 and ask the pairs to use it to plan their instructions. Provide cameras for the learners to photograph aspects of the game.
- When they've finished planning, tell the learners to write their instructions on the computer, adding their photographs or any necessary diagrams for greater clarity.

## Plenary

- Hold a table-top gallery, where each pair displays their work on their table and the rest of the class walk round looking at each other's instructions.
- Ask: *Tell me something you liked about someone else's instructions.*
- Explain that you will create a book out of the completed instructions and make it available to the other learners in the school.

### Success criteria

Ask the learners:

- Which ideas for good instructions did you include?
- Explain the layout of an instructional text.
- How did using photographs in these instructions help make them better?
- Which imperative verbs did you use in this type of instructions?

### Ideas for differentiation

**Support:** Support these learners as they choose a suitable game and talk through the game together before they start planning. Provide them with the vocabulary on photocopiable page 38.

**Extension:** Ask these learners to carefully consider their audience when making their language choices.

Name: _____

# Game instructions

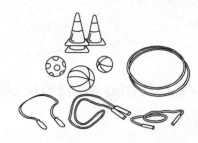

| Title: | How to play: _____ |
|---|---|
| How many people?<br>What equipment?<br>How much space? | You will need:<br><br>● _____<br><br>● _____<br><br>● _____<br><br>● _____<br><br>● _____<br><br>● _____ |
| What to do: | ● First,<br><br>● _____<br><br>● _____<br><br>● _____<br><br>● _____<br><br>● _____<br><br>● _____<br><br>● _____<br><br>● _____ |
| Safety warning: | _____<br><br>_____<br><br>_____ |

 *Cambridge Primary: Ready to Go Lessons for English Stage 3* © Hodder & Stoughton Ltd 2013

# Recipes

## Learning objectives

- Establish purpose for writing, using features and style based on model texts. (3Wn2)
- Consider ways that information is set out on page and on screen, e.g. lists, charts, bullet points. (3Rn4)

## Resources

Flour; milk; egg; butter; banana; honey; scales; spoon; knife; bowl; electric whisk; fish slice; frying pan; heat source; camera; photocopiable page 44; scissors; paper; computers; range of children's cookery books; printer.

## Starter

- Make banana pancakes using the recipe on photocopiable page 44 (reordered), instructing the learners to help with each stage, but conceal the recipe from them.
- Take some photographs of the process as you go along and make these photographs available to the learners in the Main activity.
- This activity could be reworked using a non-cook recipe if necessary.

## Main activities

- Distribute photocopiable page 44 to the learners and display an enlarged version.
- Read through the recipe. Ask: *Is everything there?* (Yes, but not displayed clearly and not in the right order.)
- Tell the learners to cut out and sort the information on the photocopiable page to create recipe instructions. Ask them to bear in mind all that they have learnt about instructions to create a clear and attractive pancake recipe on a fresh piece of paper or on the computer.
- Make a range of cookery books available and ask the learners to look through them for presentation ideas.
- Tell the learners that whilst they might like to use some of the elements from the photocopiable page, you will hope to see them changing and improving some of the elements.

- Ask: *What are you going to do first? Should all of the pictures be used?* (No, and the learners could use their own if they prefer.) *Where in the instructions would pictures be most helpful to the reader? Do you need to add any illustrations?*
- Make the photographs from the Starter activity available to the learners.

## Plenary

- Ask the learners to swap their recipe instructions with a partner and role-play following them to check that they work.
- Model giving two stars and a wish (two things you are happy with and one objective to extend the learning), for example:
  - *I like the way you have used labels on the pictures.*
  - *You have got the instructions in the correct order.*
  - *Next time, space out the ingredients to make them easier to read.*

## Success criteria

Ask the learners:

- Why are pictures useful in a recipe?
- What kind of words tell us to do something in a recipe?
- How is the information set out on the page?
- Why is it important to get recipe instruction in the right order?

## Ideas for differentiation

**Support:** Ask these learners to use role-play to act out the recipe to check they have organised it correctly.

**Extension:** Challenge these learners to create the recipe without using the photocopiable page.

# Banana pancakes

Use the pictures and information below to create a set of instructions for making banana pancakes.

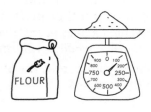 

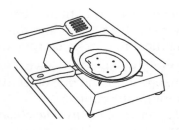 

You will need: 125 g flour, 150 ml milk, 1 egg, a knob of butter, 1 banana, a dollop of honey

Safety: Ask an adult to help with the cooking using a hot pan.

Serve with sliced banana and honey.

Melt a small amount of butter in a frying pan.

Whisk the flour, milk and egg together until you get a smooth batter.

Weigh out all the dry ingredients.

Pour a small amount of the batter into the hot pan.

Cook the pancake for approximately 2 minutes on each side.

*Cambridge Primary: Ready to Go Lessons for English Stage 3* © Hodder & Stoughton Ltd 2013

# Planning instructions

Learning objectives

- Establish purpose for writing, using features and style based on model texts. (3Wn2)
- Consider ways that information is set out on page and on screen, e.g. lists, charts, bullet points. (3Rn4)
- Write first-person accounts and descriptions based on observation. (3Wf1)

### Resources

Photocopiable pages 46 and 48; soft toy animals; washing-up bowls; pet shampoo; towel; cameras; printer.

## Starter

- Ask: *What features do we find in a good set of instructions?* Display photocopiable page 48 and check that the learners mention everything on the list.
- Establish why we have success criteria and why they are important, discussing the impact of different elements.

## Main activities

- Explain to the learners that you are going to visit your grandmother and she wants you to bath her pet. You haven't done it before so you wondered if they would help you write some instructions on how to bath a pet.
- Give the learners time to think about how they will approach the problem by discussing it with a talk partner.
- Model pretending to bath your toy animal but make some deliberate mistakes, for example lift the animal out of the washing up bowl and pretend he is dripping water everywhere: *I forgot the towel!*
- As the learners start to spot the errors, ask for some suggestions as to the best way to start. Ask: *What should I do?*
- Distribute and display an enlarged version of photocopiable page 46 and discuss with the learners how the frame could help ensure they include all the details necessary.

- Tell the learners to work in pairs and begin planning their own set of instructions. Provide toys and bowls and encourage the learners to role-play the task first, taking photographs at each stage. This will give them an opportunity to sequence the events correctly, choose appropriate vocabulary and have photographs to use in their finished set of instructions.
- Provide the learners with photocopiable page 46 to plan out their set of instructions.

## Plenary

- Choose one of the pairs of learners to begin reading their plan while another pair follows the instructions to check they work.
- Give all of the learners the opportunity to read their plan to another pair who follow the instructions.
- Look back at the success criteria on photocopiable page 48. Have they included everything?

### Success criteria

Ask the learners:

- Which imperative verbs have you chosen for these instructions?
- Is there any additional information needed in these instructions? (Wear an apron? Do it outside? Check the water is not too hot?)
- Change the following instruction into one that uses an imperative verb: 'You might want to give your animal a little cuddle before you put him in the water.' (Reassure your animal and then place him in the water.)

### Ideas for differentiation

**Support:** Provide these learners with copies of their photographs to sequence before planning their instructions.

**Extension:** Challenge these learners to choose another procedure, for example how to clean out a fish tank.

Name: _____

# Instructions planning frame

**Title:**

**You will need:**

- _____
- _____
- _____
- _____

**What to do**

(Use this section to get your instructions in the right order and don't forget the bossy verbs!)

1. _____

2. _____

3. _____

4. _____

5. _____

6. _____

7. _____

8. _____

**Pictures and diagrams:**

- What are they going to be?

  _____

- Where will you put them?

  _____

- Any other information needed?

  _____

*Cambridge Primary: Ready to Go Lessons for English Stage 3* © Hodder & Stoughton Ltd 2013

# Writing instructions

## Learning objectives

● Establish purpose for writing, using features and style based on model texts. (3Wn2)

● Consider ways that information is set out on page and on screen, e.g. lists, charts, bullet points. (3Rn4)

## Resources

Photocopiable page 46 and 48; print-outs of the photographs taken during the last lesson; scissors; glue; large pieces of paper.

## Starter

• Explain to the learners that they are going to check that their plans for their 'How to wash your pet' instructions are detailed enough by programming a robot (a partner) to follow them.

• Explain that the robot can only do exactly what they have been told or **programmed** to do.

• Model this by asking one of the learners to read out their instructions and follow them, using jerky movements and only doing exactly what the instructions say. Explain that this should make them fool proof!

• Give the learners a few minutes to try this with a partner, then swap over so both get to check their plans.

• Ask: *Has anyone needed to change their instructions to improve them?*

## Main activities

• Display some of the printed photographs from the previous lesson. Ask: *How can we use these? Do we need to use them all?* Discuss with the learners that they need to be selective, otherwise the instructions will be too cluttered and difficult to follow.

• Distribute the success criteria (photocopiable page 48) and display an enlarged version. Discuss each section, giving the learners the opportunity to be clear about the success criteria.

• Explain to the learners that it is very important these instructions are complete and very clear. Hand out the large pieces of paper and tell the learners that they will need to fill them with the instructions.

• Remind the learners that the best instructions will have followed the success criteria and have different sections that have been spaced out evenly, making them easy to read and follow.

• Ask the learners to write their instructions.

• When they've finished, ask them to check their instructions against the success criteria and then swap with a partner to check each other's work against the criteria.

## Plenary

• Organise a table-top gallery, where all the learners lay out their instructions on the tables and everyone gets the opportunity to see each other's work.

• Ask: *What have you see that was good? What made some instructions stand out more than others?*

## Success criteria

Ask the learners:

● What sort of layout and presentation did you need to think about?

● Are the instructions fit for the purpose? Do they work?

● Where might you find these kinds of instructions? Who would read them?

● Why are these kinds of instructions better written down?

## Ideas for differentiation

**Support:** Ask these learners to present their instructions in a flowchart using a sequence of photographs taken during role-playing the task.

**Extension:** Remind these learners to consider their audience when choosing their vocabulary.

Name: _____

# Success criteria for instructions

Use this form to check your set of instructions. Ask your partner to check them too.

| Success criteria | Author | Partner |
|---|---|---|
| I have included a title ('How to …'). | | |
| I have included a list of the things needed with bullet points. | | |
| I have used a clear, easy-to-read layout. | | |
| I have included good pictures or diagrams. | | |
| I have written my instructions in the right order with numbers or bullet points. | | |
| I have used these 'bossy' imperative verbs: | | |
| I have checked my use of capital letters and full stops. | | |

*Cambridge Primary: Ready to Go Lessons for English Stage 3* © Hodder & Stoughton Ltd 2013

# Unit assessment

## Questions to ask

- Where might we find instructions?
- What features would you find in instructions?
- Do good instructions have to have diagrams and pictures? Explain your answer.
- Explain what an imperative verb is and how they are used in instructions.

- What should the layout of good instructions be like?
- Give oral instructions on how to find the hall, dining room or headteacher's office.

## Summative assessment activities

Listen to and observe the learners during these activities and you will be able to identify those who appear to be confident and those who may need additional support.

### Problem recipe

**You will need:**

Photocopiable page 50.

**What to do**

- Distribute an enlarged copy of photocopiable page 50 to the learners in groups of three to four and ask them to edit it. (Hopefully they will see that it needs clearer imperatives and shorter sentences.)

### Oral directions

This game helps the learners to choose the most clear and simple language for directions to avoid confusion.

**You will need:**

A variety of ordinary classroom objects placed around the room so they are visible, e.g. pencil, chair, reading book, water bottle, Science book, dictionary, coloured pencils, counting beads; a list of all the objects you've gathered.

**What to do**

- Display the list of objects and ask the learners to work in pairs.
- Ask one learner from each pair to choose an item from the list, keeping the item secret from their partner.
- Tell those learners to direct their partner to the object by giving only oral instructions, for example: 'Walk to the window.', 'Turn to face the teacher's desk.', 'Put your hand on the teacher's chair.' (The chair was the object.)
- They may only give each instruction once, so they will need to use short simple sentences and clear language.
- The learners have to get to the object but not necessarily in the shortest time – it is not a race!
- When their partner has reached the object, ask them to swap over.

## Written assessment

- Display these instructions as a list and read them together:
  - Choose a snack or drink you know how to make.
  - Use the planning frame to organise your ideas.
  - Check your plan against the success criteria.
  - Create your instructions.
  - When you think you have finished, check the success criteria again!
- Distribute photocopiable pages 46 and 48 and ask the learners to work independently to follow the instructions.

Name: _____

# Writing instructions

These instructions are not quite right. Can you make them better by crossing out and rewriting parts of the text, or adding new text?

### How to make maple syrup eggy bread

You will need:

- Two slices of bread
- One egg
- 1 tablespoon of maple syrup
- Oil for frying

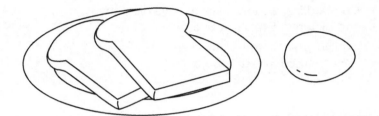

1.  After you have washed your hands, wearing an apron.

2.  Using a fork or maybe a whisk gently beat the egg in a bowl.

3.  Put the slices of bread on to a chopping board and cut them in half diagonally.

4.  If you pick up each slice and dip it into the egg making sure both sides are coated then leave all the slices in the bowl so all the egg mixture is soaked into the bread.

5.  While the bread and egg are soaking, put a frying pan on over a medium heat and pour in oil.

6.  You cook the slices of bread by gently placing them into the pan.

6.  Use one of those flat things to turn them over after a few minutes or until they are more golden.

7.  It looks nice on the plate if you stack the triangles then drizzle the maple syrup over.

8.  Take a step back and admire your work then eat!

It might be a good idea to ask an adult to help you using the frying pan and to do the cooking part.

*Cambridge Primary: Ready to Go Lessons for English Stage 3* © Hodder & Stoughton Ltd 2013

# Patterns in poems

## Learning objectives

● Read a range of story, poetry and information books and begin to make links between them. (3Rf9)
● Read aloud with expression to engage the listener. (3Rf2)
● Practise learning and reciting poems. (3Rf12)

## Resources

Photocopiable pages 52 and 53; internet access; coloured pens; a variety of poetry anthologies or pre-prepared collections of poems.

## Starter

• Display an enlarged version of photocopiable page 52 and read the two poems to the learners.
• Talk briefly about the rhyming patterns in both poems.
• Share some examples of poems with rhyming couplets, for example 'I taught my cat to clean my room' by Kenn Nesbitt at www.poetry4kids.com/poem-156.html, or alternate rhyming lines, for example 'All my great excuses' by Kenn Nesbitt at www.poetry4kids.com/poem-349.html.

## Main activities

• Explain to the learners that they are going to look for patterns in poems. Together, draw up a list of the types of patterns they might find in poems, for example:
  • rhyme
  • rhythm
  • alliteration
  • repeated phrases or lines
  • structure of the verse / stanza.
• Discuss how these devices create different effects for the reader. Look again at the two displayed poems. Ask: *What patterns can you see in these poems?*
• Using coloured pens, underline the rhyming words in the two poems and discuss the rhyme structures used in each one.

• Ask: *Can you see any other patterns?* Discuss the use of time in 'Scissors' and how it structures the poem. Look at the use of the repeated word 'water' in 'Water everywhere'.
• Leave the list of patterns displayed and distribute photocopiable page 53 and a variety of poetry anthologies or pre-prepared collections of poems. Ask the learners to work in pairs to choose a handful of poems with patterns to look at further. Tell the learners to use the table to collect patterns from the poems they read and to express their views about them.

## Plenary

• Ask the learners to work with a partner and pick a favourite verse or whole poem to learn off by heart and share with another pair. The poem or verse must contain a pattern that the learners can explain to another pair.
• Choose a few pairs of learners to share their examples with the rest of the class.

## Success criteria

Ask the learners:

● What kinds of patterns can you find in poems?
● Explain what alliteration is.
● How did the patterns change the way you read the poems aloud?
● What effect does the reader get from the patterns in poetry?
● Why is it a good idea to read a poem a few times?

## Ideas for differentiation

**Support:** Provide these learners with copies of a few suitable poems to write on and annotate as modelled in the Main activity.

**Extension:** Challenge these learners to collect an anthology of poems with each pattern.

# Patterns in poems

## Water Everywhere

There's water on the ceiling,
And water on the wall,
There's water in the bathroom,
And water in the hall,
There's water on the landing,
And water on the stair,
Whenever Daddy takes a bath
There's water everywhere.

Valerie Bloom

## Scissors

Nobody leave the room.
Everyone listen to me.
We had ten-pair of scissors
At half-past two,
And now there's only three.

We really need those scissors,
That's what makes me mad.
If it was seven pairs
Of children we'd lost,
It wouldn't be so bad.

Seven pairs of scissors,
Disappeared from sight.
Not one of you leaves
Till we find them.
We can stop here all night!

I don't want to hear excuses.
Don't anyone speak.
Just ransack this room
Till we find them,
Or we'll stop here … all week!

Scissors don't lose themselves,
Melt away or explode.
Scissors have not got
Legs of their own
To go running off up the road.

Allan Ahlberg

Name: _____

# Finding patterns in poems

Complete the table below with examples from poems you have read.

| Name of poem and poet | Patterns | What is good? |
|---|---|---|
| 'Scissors' by Allan Ahlberg | Rhyming 2nd and 5th lines | I like the picture of a classroom I get in my head. |
| 'Water everywhere' by Valerie Bloom | Rhyming pattern:<br><br>Repeated word:<br><br>_____ | |
| | | |
| | | |
| | | |
| | | |

# Expressing opinions on poetry

### Learning objectives

- Listen and respond appropriately to others' views and opinions. (3SL4)
- Read aloud with expression to engage the listener. (3Rf2)
- Take turns in discussion, building on what others have said. (3SL3)

### Resources

Photocopiable pages 55 and 56; a variety of poems around the theme of the senses.

## Starter

- Distribute photocopiable page 55 and read the poem together with the learners.
- Display the following questions and ask the learners to discuss their answers with a partner:
  - 'What patterns can you notice?'
  - 'What do you like / dislike about the poem?'
  - 'How does the poem make you feel or think?'
  - 'Which words and phrases did you enjoy? Why?'
  - 'Why is the last verse a bit cheeky?'

## Main activities

- Display an enlarged copy of photocopiable page 56 and model using the learners' responses to the poem to fill it in, for example:
  - 'I like that the poem is light-hearted, simple to understand and funny.'
  - 'It makes me think about my senses.'
  - 'It paints pictures of foods with nasty tastes and smells.'
  - 'I like the phrase "things that frighten other noses" because it's funny.'
  - 'I like the way it is a bit cheeky, and surprising.'
  - 'There is a pattern of pairs of alternate rhyming couplets (the second and fourth lines rhyme).'
- Organise the learners into small groups of three or four, and give each group photocopiable page 56. Distribute a different poem about the senses to each group.

- Ask them to read their poem aloud and then discuss it. Tell them to elect a scribe to write down on the photocopiable page the ideas the group come up with.
- Remind the learners that responses to poetry are personal, so as long as one of the group can justify what they think, their thoughts can be added to the appropriate box.
- Give the learners time to read aloud and discuss their poem, then rotate the poems around the class so that each group discusses four poems. With each rotation, provide the groups with a new copy of photocopiable page 56.

## Plenary

- Give each group of learners an opportunity to feed back on their discussions and compare their thoughts.
- Question the learners' responses to get them to begin justifying them.
- Ask the leaners what they have learnt about working in a group. Ask: *Did you work well? What was difficult? How could you make the group work better next time?*

### Success criteria

Ask the learners:

- What can you tell me about the poems you have read today?
- How have you engaged the listener when reading the poems?
- What sort of poetry do you enjoy reading?
- Which poems painted a picture in your mind? How do you think the poet achieved that?

### Ideas for differentiation

**Support:** Provide an adult helper to work with these learners and to scribe all the ideas and opinions.

**Extension:** Give these learners an opportunity to collect poems on a similar theme.

# My Senses All are Backward

My senses all are backward
and it really makes me wonder
if on the day that I was born
somebody made a blunder.

For, strange but true, my senses
all got totally reversed.
Now everything I like the best
is what you'd call the worst.

I only like the smell of things
that frighten other noses.
I love the odor of a skunk.
I hate the smell of roses.

I only like the taste of foods
that cause most folks to shiver.
I hate the taste of chocolate.
I'm crazy over liver.

I'm not too fond of music
but there's simply no denying
I like the sound of honking horns
and little babies crying.

I hate the feel of silky, velvet
softness on my skin.
I much prefer the way it feels
when sitting on a pin.

I hate the look of anything
that's really cute and snuggly.
The things I think are pretty
are what most consider ugly.

So let me tell you one more thing
before I have to go:
I think YOU are the most attractive
person that I know.

Kenn Nesbitt

Name: _____

# Identifying features in poems

Use this table to record your thoughts about a poem you have read.

Name of poem: _____

by _____

| | |
|---|---|
| 1. What do you like or dislike about the poem? _____ _____ _____ _____ _____ | 2. How does the poem make you think or feel? _____ _____ _____ _____ _____ |
| 3. Does the poem paint any pictures in your mind? _____ _____ _____ _____ _____ | 4. Which words and phrases do you enjoy? Why? _____ _____ _____ _____ _____ |
| 5. What patterns have you noticed? _____ _____ _____ _____ | 6. What other interesting things could you say about the poem (e.g. entertaining, funny)? _____ _____ _____ _____ |

 *Cambridge Primary: Ready to Go Lessons for English Stage 3* © Hodder & Stoughton Ltd 2013

# Planning and writing a poem

- Write and perform poems, attending to the sound of words. (3Wf9)
- Use ICT to write, edit and present work. (3Wp4)
- Read aloud with expression to engage the listener. (3Rf2)

Photocopiable pages 56 and 58; *We're Going on a Bear Hunt* by Michael Rosen (Walker Books); internet access; video cameras.

## Starter

- Read *We're Going on a Bear Hunt* by Michael Rosen to the learners. Watch Michael Rosen reciting it at www.youtube.com/watch?v=ytc0U2WAz4s.
- Display an enlarged version of photocopiable page 56 and fill in the boxes for *We're Going on a Bear Hunt*. Read each question in turn and allow the learners time to discuss their ideas with a partner before gathering thoughts from the class.

## Main activities

- Pass round your copy of *We're Going on a Bear Hunt* for the learners to look at, so that they know what the poem looks like written down.
- Tell them that they are going to write a new version of the poem and that they can make as many or as few changes as they like, for example they could change:
  - the bear to a different animal or something else scary
  - some of the obstacles
  - just one verse or the whole poem.
- Distribute photocopiable page 58 and discuss with the learners how the writing frame will help them. Encourage them to try out different ideas and then choose the ones that work best.

- If you would like to create a class version, choose an animal or scary creature for the whole class to work on. Then ask the learners to work in groups to develop a verse each, which can be combined to create a class poem.
- When each group is happy with their verse, or each learner is happy with their whole poem, ask them to write out a final version and practise reading it.
- Provide the learners with video cameras to record a performance of their new poem in the style of Michael Rosen's performance.

## Plenary

- Watch the finished recordings and model giving oral feedback on the performance. If possible, provide an opportunity for the learners to perform their poem/s to an audience.
- If the learners have written separate poems, collect in the written versions and put them together in a book to share with other classes.

Ask the learners:

- What strategies and language choices did you use to engage the listener?
- What changes did you make to the original poem?
- How did you decide which ideas were the best ones?
- How did you feel performing the poem?

**Support:** Ask these learners to use the writing frame to change only the animal.

**Extension:** Tell these learners that they need to consider the vocabulary choices Michael Rosen made when creating their version of the poem.

Name: _____

# We're going on a turkey hunt

We're going on a _____ hunt.

We're going on a _____ hunt.
We're going to catch a big one.
What a beautiful day!
We're not scared.

Uh-uh _____

_____

We can't go over it.
We can't go under it.

Oh no!
We've got to go through it!

_____

_____

 *Cambridge Primary: Ready to Go Lessons for English Stage 3* © Hodder & Stoughton Ltd 2013

# Features of a play-script

- Read play-scripts and dialogue, with awareness of different voices. (3Rf11)
- Practise to improve performance when reading aloud. (3SL6)

Photocopiable page 60; multiple copies of a short play.

## Starter

- Distribute photocopiable page 60. Ask the learners to look at the layout and discuss with a partner the basic conventions of a play-script, giving them time to locate the various elements.
- Together, capture the play-script features used in the extract:
  - the layout – the characters' names down the left side, and the dialogue indented
  - the punctuation – speech marks are unnecessary
  - the stage directions – the setting is introduced; directions are used to say how something should be said or done.

## Main activities

- Explain to the learners that to be able to read a play they must understand the conventions and rules, otherwise it will not make any sense.
- Ask them to mark and annotate the key features of a play-script as discussed in the Starter activity on their copy of photocopiable page 60.
- Distribute copies of a short play, for example *The Twits: Plays for Children* by Roald Dahl, adapted by David Wood (Puffin). Allocate the learners in small groups a scene each.
- Tell the learners to read through their scene, allocating parts amongst themselves. If you are using a play other than *The Twits*, help them to see how the play-script conventions have been used.

- Give the learners time to practise their scene a few times so they become familiar with the words and more confident with the stage directions. They should mime any props needed.
- Ask each group to perform their scenes in turn until the play is completed.

## Plenary

- If possible, ask one group of learners to perform to the rest of the class, and provide a 'stage' at the front for them.
- Ask: *What worked well in the good performances?*
- Discuss with the learners the difference between reading the play-script the first time and then the last time. Ask: *What got easier? Why did it get easier?*

Ask the learners:

- What are the differences between a story and a play-script? Give some examples.
- How can you tell who is speaking in a play-script?
- Why is it a good idea to read the play-script a few times? How did the performance improve?

**Support:** Let these learners work in pairs, doubling up on the reading parts to increase confidence.

**Extension:** Explain to these learners that they need to focus on the stage directions and make their performance as polished as possible.

# Features of a play-script

**Meet the Twits**

NARRATOR: Mr and Mrs Twit were a truly disgusting couple who enjoyed playing nasty tricks on one another. One night, when Mrs Twit was asleep, Mr Twit put a slimy frog under her bedclothes. To pay him back, Mrs Twit put squiggly worms in Mr Twit's spaghetti. But sometimes they had grander, even nastier ideas ...

(Curtain up, revealing MR and MRS TWIT)

One day, Mr Twit announced...

MR TWIT:     I've been thinking.

MRS TWIT:   Did it hurt?

MR TWIT:     I am going ...

MRS TWIT:   The further the better!

MR TWIT:     I am going to run a circus!

MRS TWIT:   To what, you twit?

MR TWIT:     To run a circus!

MRS TWIT:   Run a circus? You couldn't run an egg-and-spoon race.

MR TWIT:     You wait, you old trout. (*Grandly*) I will train animals.

MRS TWIT:   Animals, what animals?

MR TWIT:     (*After a pause for thought*) Monkeys!

MRS TWIT:   Monkeys? Where will you find monkeys?

Roald Dahl, adapted by David Wood

# Planning a play-script

- Write simple play-scripts based on reading. (3Wf4)
- Read play-scripts and dialogue, with awareness of different voices. (3Rf11)
- Practise to improve performance when reading aloud. (3SL6)

*The Twits* by Roald Dahl (Puffin); large pieces of paper; photocopiable pages 62 and 63.

## Starter

- Read aloud the first few chapters of *The Twits* by Roald Dahl (Puffin). This provides some useful background information about the main characters. (They are pretty horrid and play nasty tricks on each other all the time.)
- Collect on large pieces of paper the learners' ideas about what the Twits are like, encouraging them to give evidence from the text.

## Main activities

- Ask the learners to work with a partner to role-play what happens when Mrs Twit serves up spaghetti with wriggly worms to Mr Twit. Encourage them to enjoy getting into character.
- Now, ask the learners to think of a new scene with a new trick played on one of the characters by the other. Provide the learners with photocopiable page 62 to record their ideas. Encourage the learners not to do anything too nasty!
- When the learners have decided on a new trick, they need to role-play it in character to see how it works and what needs to go into their plan. Encourage them to repeat this several times to get the scene clear in their heads, which will make it easier to write the play-script later.

- Distribute photocopiable page 63 and model how to use photocopiable page 62 to help the learners complete the writing frame.
- Remind the learners to write the name of the character speaking in the left column and what they say in the right, leaving an empty line between each new speaker. They may need a fresh copy of photocopiable page 63 or another piece of paper for editing and alterations.

## Plenary

- Ask the learners to swap their photocopiable page 63 with another pair to check for mistakes and for anything that needs changing.
- Give the learners an opportunity to make alterations.

Ask the learners:

- How did you set the scene?
- What are the key features of turning a role-play into a play-script?
- How did it help to act out the play before trying to write the ideas down?
- What sort of suggestions could you make to improve the play?

**Support:** Organise these learners to work with an adult helper who can scribe and help them organise their ideas. Encourage them to keep the plot simple.

**Extension:** Ask these learners to consider the staging of the play and how to explain this in their script.

Name: _____

# Planning a play

Use this table to collect your ideas for a new scene for **The Twits**.

| Ideas for a trick: | Ideas for a setting: |
|---|---|
| _____ | _____ |
| _____ | _____ |
| _____ | _____ |
| _____ | _____ |

Ideas for the plot:

_____

_____

_____

_____

_____

Draw a simple sketch of how the play will look.
Include any props that you need.

*Cambridge Primary: Ready to Go Lessons for English Stage 3* © Hodder & Stoughton Ltd 2013

Name: _____

# Play-script planning frame

Use this template to plan your play-script.

Scene title: _____

Characters: _____

_____

_____

Stage directions: _____

| Character | Dialogue |
|---|---|
|  |  |
|  |  |
|  |  |
|  |  |
|  |  |
|  |  |
|  |  |
|  |  |
|  |  |
|  |  |
|  |  |
|  |  |
|  |  |
|  |  |
|  |  |

# Writing a play-script

## Learning objectives

● Write simple play-scripts based on reading. (3Wf4)

● Read play-scripts and dialogue, with awareness of different voices. (3Rf11)

● Identify misspelt words in own writing and keep individual spelling logs. (3PSV10)

## Resources

Photocopiable pages 60, 63 (completed) and 65; writing books or computers.

## Starter

• Ask the learners: *What success criteria should we be using for writing a play?*

• Display an enlarged version of photocopiable page 60 and collect the learners' ideas for layout features that a good play-script should have.

• Pay close attention to the details, for example a colon after the characters' names, the sort of information that is in brackets, and so on.

## Main activities

• Explain to the learners that they are going to use their notes and first draft (photocopiable page 63) to write their play-script, and that the best play-scripts will include the features from the success criteria.

• Hand out photocopiable page 65 and discuss the success criteria with the learners, pointing out examples or evidence in the shared text from the Starter activity:
  • title of the scene
  • names of the characters with a colon after the name
  • punctuation to help the reader choose the right tone: question marks, exclamation marks, and so on
  • the words the character says
  • stage directions, in brackets, to show what the actors are doing or where they are
  • correct spellings
  • full stops and capital letters.

• Ask the learners to write out the final version of their play-script (in their writing books, on the computer or on a new copy of photocopiable page 63), checking it against the success criteria as they go.

• Ask the learners to give their finished play-script to a partner, who should give it a further check against the success criteria.

## Plenary

• Discuss the performance side of reading this type of text: projecting your voice, not turning your back on the audience, using props, and so on.

• Give each pair of learners the opportunity to perform their scene to a suitable audience.

• Finally, ask the learners to tell you what they have learnt about writing a play-script and what they have enjoyed.

## Success criteria

Ask the learners:

● What would you write if you wanted a character to say something angrily?

● What checks have you made to improve your play-script?

● How did you check your spellings?

● How did you ensure your play-script was easy to follow and use?

## Ideas for differentiation

**Support:** Ask these learners to follow the style of photocopiable page 60 to help them organise their ideas.

**Extension:** Encourage these learners to look at other examples of a play-script to identify how the different features of a play-script can be interpreted.

Name: _____

# Play-script success criteria

Have you remembered all the rules for writing play-scripts?
Check your play-script against these success criteria.
Ask your partner to check your play-script, too.

| Success criteria | Author | Partner |
|---|---|---|
| Title of the scene | | |
| Names of the characters with a colon after the name | | |
| Punctuation to help the reader choose the right tone (e.g. ? or !) | | |
| The words the character says | | |
| Stage directions, in brackets, to show what the actors are doing or where they are | | |
| Correct spellings | | |
| Full stops and capital letters | | |
| An empty line between each new person speaking | | |

# Unit assessment

- Explain the sorts of patterns you might find in a poem.
- Why do poets use poetic devices and patterns? What effects do they have on the reader?
- Describe the main differences between a play-script and a narrative. How do you recognise one from the other?

- 'Play-scripts are hard to read on your own.' Explain why someone might say this.
- How do you know how to say a character's lines in a play? What clues are there to help you?
- Which is better, a play-script or a narrative? Why?

## Summative assessment activities

Observe the learners while they play these games. You will quickly be able to identify those who appear to be confident and those who may need additional support.

### Technical vocabulary card sort

This game helps the learners to use the correct terminology for writing and performing play-scripts.

**You will need:**

Photocopiable page 67; scissors; a variety of dictionaries.

**What to do**

- Organise the learners into groups of four and give each group photocopiable page 67 and a pair of scissors.
- Explain that the words on the left are all to do with plays and play-scripts, while the right-hand column has the definitions, but they are all muddled up.
- Tell the learners to cut out the words and definitions and work together to match up the words with their correct meaning.
- The groups can check their definitions at the end using dictionaries.

### Spot the pattern

This is a useful activity for assessing the learners' understanding of patterns in poems.

**You will need:**

A selection of poetry anthologies; a stopwatch.

**What to do**

- Divide the learners into groups of about four.
- Distribute a selection of poems or anthologies to each group.
- Ask the learners in each group to take turns to find a poem and read it aloud to their group.
- The other members of the group need to listen out for poetic patterns, making a list of any they hear.
- When the first person has finished reading, the next group member can start.
- Give the groups three minutes to collect as many patterns as they can. The winning team will be the one that has collected the most patterns at the end of the three minutes.

Ask the learners to create a poster to explain the key features of a play-script, or the main differences between a play-script and a narrative. The learners are to work independently for this task.

# Technical vocabulary

Cut out these words and meanings and match them up correctly.

| | |
|---|---|
| Play: | People who act out the parts of the characters in the play-script. |
| Play-script: | People in the play-script. |
| Narrator: | Background to show where the scene is set. |
| Actors: | Clothes for actors. |
| Characters: | A story told by actors on a stage. |
| Acts: | Place of action. |
| Scene: | Objects needed for the play. |
| Scenery: | Someone who tells or recounts the story. |
| Stage: | Chapters in a play. |
| Props: | Where the drama or action is happening. |
| Costumes: | A script written for a play. |

# Unit 2A: Myths, legends and fables

## Traditional tales

● Identify different types of stories and typical story themes. (3Rf5)

● Read a range of story, poetry and information books and begin to make links between them. (3Rf9)

● Answer questions with some reference to single points in a text. (3Rf3)

Photocopiable pages 69 and 70; map or globe; collections of myths and legends from around the world; internet access.

## Starter

● Read the first paragraph of photocopiable page 69 to the learners. Discuss how this would originally have been an oral story.

● Identify the part of the world the story comes from on a map or globe.

● Read the rest of photocopiable pages 69 and 70, pausing to discuss any unfamiliar language.

## Main activities

● Ask the learners to turn to a partner and discuss their responses to the story, picking out details where possible. Ask them to discuss:
  ● *What is the theme of the story?*
  ● *Who are the main characters?*
  ● *What is the setting?*
  ● *What sort of pictures did you get in your head?*
  ● *Is the story really a legend?*
(Create a version of the table at the top of the next column on the board where the learners can see it.)

● Ask the learners to work with a partner to read other myths and legends from around the world in books or online (for example at http://myths.e2bn.org/mythsandlegends/).

● Encourage them to note any stories that share features with 'The Legend of the Three Sisters'.

● Ask them to choose a story to share with the rest of the class.

| Legends | Myths |
|---|---|
| ● Often loosely based on a true event in the past. | ● Stories often thousands of years old. |
| ● The hero was or could have been a real person. | ● Sometimes they explain an event that at the time people did not understand, for example a terrible flood or earthquake. |
| ● Story has passed down the generations. | |
| ● Normally there is an associated meaning for the region in which it is set. | ● Sometimes explain how something came to be. |

## Plenary

● Ask the learners in pairs to read their chosen story aloud, and as a class discuss:
  ● *How did you feel about the story?*
  ● *What is the theme of the story?*
  ● *Is it a myth or legend?*

Ask the learners:

● What can you tell me about myths and legends?

● Are they true stories?

● What sort of themes do you usually find in myths and legends?

● What similarities are there between the myths and legends you have been reading?

**Support:** Organise these learners to work in a small adult-helper led group, to explain any unfamiliar vocabulary.

**Extension:** Ask these learners to create a table to organise their ideas about whether the story is a myth or legend.

# The Legend of the Three Sisters

In Australia, the mysterious Blue Mountains tower high above lush rainforests and deep valleys. In the area where the Gundungurra people lived, there rises an outcrop topped by three rocky formations, known as the Three Sisters. This is the story of how they came to be there.

Long, long ago, the mystical land of Gondwana was beautiful, peaceful and untouched. In Gondwana, there lived Tyawan, a Clever Man of the Gundungurra people. He had three daughters called Meenhi, Wimlah and Gunnedoo, whom he treasured above all else.

In a deep hole in the valley there lived a Bunyip: a huge, evil creature who loved to feast on human flesh, particularly that of young girls and women. Its cry was harsh and horrible and if you heard it, the only safe thing to do was run away as quickly as possible. Everyone feared the Bunyip.

If you needed to pass its hole, it was important to creep very quietly so that it was not disturbed.

When Tyawan had to pass the hole, he would leave his daughters safely on the cliff above behind a rocky wall – just in case!

One day, waving goodbye to his daughters, he descended the cliff steps down towards the path near the Bunyip's hole. While the girls were waiting and chatting on top of the cliff, a huge centipede suddenly appeared. Startled, Meenhi screamed, jumped up, picked up a stone and threw it at the centipede.

# The Legend of the Three Sisters (continued)

The stone missed the centipede, but rolled over the edge of the cliff and, picking up speed, crashed into the valley below. The sound echoed all around the mountains. Birds, animals and even fairies stopped still as the rocks behind the three sisters shook and split open, leaving them perched together on a thin ledge.

The Bunyip, angry at being awakened, roared and dragged himself through the split to see the terrified sisters cowering on the ledge. His evil eyes widened in delight at the feast before him.

Tyawan looked up and saw the Bunyip reaching for his daughters, so he pointed his magic bone at the girls and immediately turned them to stone. They would be safe there until the Bunyip had gone and then Tyawan would change them back to their former selves.

But the Bunyip, angered at being deprived of his prey, chased Tyawan through the forest and up a mountain where he found himself trapped. So Tyawan used his magic bone again and changed himself into a Lyre bird and glided away. Everyone was safe. But then, in dismay, Tyawan realised that he had dropped his bone whilst changing.

After the Bunyip had gone back to his deep dark pool, Tyawan glided down to the forest floor and searched and searched for his magic bone … where he can still be seen to this day, in the shape of the Lyre bird, scratching and searching the forest floors of the Blue Mountains, looking for his bone, calling to his daughters above and feeding on insects whilst he searches.

The Three Sisters stand silently watching him from their ledge, hoping and hoping that one day their father will find his magic bone and be able turn them back to Aboriginal girls.

http://myths.e2bn.org/mythsandlegends/textonly762-the-legend-of-the-three-sisters.html

*Cambridge Primary: Ready to Go Lessons for English Stage 3* © Hodder & Stoughton Ltd 2013

# Synonyms

- Use a dictionary or electronic means to find the spelling and meaning of words. (3PSV8)
- Generate synonyms for high frequency words, e.g. big, little, good. (3PSV14)
- Choose and compare words to strengthen the impact of writing, including noun phrases. (3Wf10)

Photocopiable page 72; thesauruses (enough for one between two learners); computers and internet access.

## Starter

- Write the words 'large' and 'huge' on the board. Ask: *What can you tell me about these two words?* Discuss the term 'synonym' (the same meaning for two different words). Ask the learners for some more pairs of synonyms, for example 'small' and 'tiny', 'warm' and 'hot' or 'pleased' and 'glad'.
- Using a thesaurus, model how you would find a synonym for 'tidy' (for example 'neat', 'organised', 'arranged', 'not messy').
- Display an enlarged version of the top half of photocopiable page 72 and read the paragraph with the learners.
- Ask: *What can you tell me about the underlined words? Could we use any synonyms to replace any of them?* Collect the learners' ideas for alternatives to the underlined words.

## Main activities

- Remind the learners that a synonym is a word with a similar meaning, therefore when a word is replaced with a synonym, the overall meaning of the sentence should not change; the effect of changing the word should be to make the description more vivid, more interesting and to draw in the reader.

- Show the learners how to use an online thesaurus (for example at www.collinsdictionary.com) or the thesaurus in a word-processing package.
- Distribute photocopiable page 72.
- Ask the learners to work with a partner and use a thesaurus, word-processing package or online thesaurus to complete the photocopiable page (finding different synonyms for the words in the passage from those suggested in the Starter).

## Plenary

- Give the learners an opportunity to feed back their synonyms, then collect the new and exciting vocabulary and display it.
- Play a quick game: put the learners into teams and challenge each team to come up with as many synonyms for 'walking' and 'shouting' as they can in 20 seconds. Who has the longest list? How many words are shared between the teams? Who has the most interesting word?

Ask the learners:

- Explain how to use a thesaurus.
- When should we think about using synonyms?
- What sort of effect does changing a word for a synonym have on the reader?

**Support:** Ask these learners to use a table to collect common synonyms using the vocabulary from the Starter.

**Extension:** Give these learners photocopiable page 70 and challenge them to work in pairs to find synonyms for words in the last two paragraphs.

Name: _____

# Synonym swap

1. Look at the underlined words. Write a synonym under each of the words / groups of words.

> In a <u>deep hole</u> in the valley there lived a Bunyip: a <u>huge, evil</u> creature
>
> who loved to <u>feast on</u> human flesh, particularly that of young girls
>
> and women. Its cry was <u>harsh and horrible</u> and if you heard it, the
>
> only safe thing to do was run away as quickly as possible. Everyone
>
> <u>feared</u> the Bunyip. If you needed to pass its hole, it was important to
>
> <u>creep very quietly</u> so that it was not disturbed.

2. Now find synonyms for these words.

| happy | | | |
|-------|--|--|--|
| afraid | | | |
| quick | | | |
| closed | | | |
| fat | | | |
| bad | | | |

3. Pick one row of synonyms and write a sentence that uses all four words.

_____

_____

*Cambridge Primary: Ready to Go Lessons for English Stage 3* © Hodder & Stoughton Ltd 2013

# Verbs and tenses

### Learning objectives

● Understand that verbs are necessary for meaning in a sentence. (3GPr5)

● Know irregular forms of common verbs. (3PSV3)

● Continue to improve consistency in the use of tenses. (3GPw4)

### Resources

Photocopiable pages 69, 70 and 74; a range of dictionaries; reading books.

## Starter

• Ask the learners to discuss with a partner what types of words they know about. After a couple of minutes, agree together that they know about verbs, nouns and adjectives.

• Write the following sentence on the board and ask the learners to identify the verbs (waiting, chatting and appeared): 'While the girls were waiting and chatting on top of the cliff, a huge centipede suddenly appeared.'

• Say: *All sentences must have a verb in them.* Ask: *Is this true?* Ask the learners to return to the story on photocopiables page 69 and 70 to test if this is true.

## Main activities

• Discuss the role verbs have in indicating when things happen:
  • past tense – 'I *moved* my bike out of the way.'
  • present tense – 'I *am moving* my bike out of the way.'
  • future tense – 'I *will move* my bike out of the way.'

• Display the words 'play', 'laugh', 'help' and 'look'. Ask: *How do we change these words into the past tense?* (Add '-ed'.)

• Now display these words: 'look', 'jump', 'throw', 'wish', 'see', 'sail' and 'wait'. Ask: *How can we put these into the present tense (the form using 'am')?* (Add '-ing'.)

• Discuss the exceptions to the rule – the irregular verbs that have to be learnt, for example 'drive' / 'drove', 'sit' / 'sat', 'take' / 'took', 'sleep' / 'slept', 'swim' / 'swam'. Ask: *Can you think of any others?*

• Distribute photocopiable page 74 and ask the learners to fill in the page using dictionaries to check their spelling.

## Plenary

• Ask the learners to discuss with a partner how to change these words into the present tense by adding '-ing': 'hop', 'beg', 'hum', 'shop'. Ask: *What happens here?* Discuss the double consonant in each case, for example 'hop' / 'hopping'.

• Now ask them to discuss how to change these words into the past tense by adding '-ed': 'hope', 'race', 'bake', 'skate'. Ask: *What happens here?* Discuss dropping the final 'e' before adding '-ed', for example 'hope' / 'hoped'.

### Success criteria

Ask the learners:

● What is a verb? When do we use verbs?

● What is meant by the past / present / future tense?

● How do verbs change depending on their tense?

● What strategies do you know to help you change the tense of a verb?

### Ideas for differentiation

**Support:** Ask these learners to use their reading books to identify verbs and then put them into a table in their past, present and future forms.

**Extension:** Encourage these learners to use what they know about synonyms to find exciting verbs that will draw in the reader, for example for 'moved' they could use 'crept', 'scuttled', 'paced' or 'wandered'.

Name: _____

# Verb tenses

1.  Fill in the missing verbs in the table below.
    The first row has been done for you.

| Past tense | Present tense | Future tense |
|---|---|---|
| I fixed | I am fixing | I will fix |
| | I am standing | |
| | | I will pull |
| I painted | | |
| | I am sliding | |

2.  Now try these.

| Past tense | Present tense | Future tense |
|---|---|---|
| I made | | |
| | | I will sing |
| | I am swimming | |
| I drank | | |

3.  Look at these sentences:

    a)  Yesterday I <u>baked</u> my favourite cookies. (past tense)

    b)  I <u>am baking</u> cakes and buns today. (present tense)

    c)  Tomorrow I <u>will bake</u> a cake for my grandmother. (future tense)

    Now use what you know about tenses of verbs to write three sentences
    of your own:

    a)  (past tense) _____

    _____

    b)  (present tense) _____

    _____

    c)  (future tense) _____

    _____

*Cambridge Primary: Ready to Go Lessons for English Stage 3* © Hodder & Stoughton Ltd 2013

# Themes, characters, settings and events

## Learning objectives

- Identify different types of stories and typical story themes. (3Rf5)
- Read a range of story, poetry and information books and begin to make links between them. (3Rf9)
- Scan a passage to find specific information and answer questions. (3Rn1)

## Resources

Photocopiable pages 69, 70, 76 and 77; collections of myths and legends in books or online; large pieces of paper; marker pens.

## Starter

- Read photocopiable page 76 to the learners.
- Ask: *Is this story a myth or a legend?*
- Briefly discuss the text with the learners, posing questions such as: *Why do you think …? What might have happened if …?*
- Encourage the learners to discuss the text with a partner and feed back to the rest of the class.

## Main activities

- Ask the learners to discuss with their partners what sort of themes, characters and settings they have found in the stories they've read in this unit. As a class, discuss the 'stock' nature of characters and settings in traditional tales and the reasons for this.
- Hand out photocopiable page 77 to the learners. Display an enlarged version and model filling it in for 'The Three Sisters' (photocopiable pages 69 and 70), using information from the text only, for example:
  - characters – loving father, trusting daughters, evil Bunyip
  - setting – a cliff near a monster
  - events – the father tries to protect his daughters; he succeeds but their lives are ruined
  - themes – love and loss; overprotection.

- Read 'Two Fast Runners' (photocopiable page 76) a second time, asking the learners to make notes on photocopiable page 77 as you read.
- Ask them to repeat this with two other myths or legends they have read or are familiar with.

## Plenary

- Split the class into four groups and allocate each group one of the headings on photocopiable page 77. Ask the groups to draw together all the information that they have written on their photocopiable pages and discuss what it tells them about myths and legends, writing down their ideas on a large piece of paper.
- Ask the groups to rotate around the room to the next group's page and add their ideas to that page. Continue until all the groups have fed back on each page.
- Display all four pages and discuss the conclusions the class has drawn.

## Success criteria

Ask the learners:

- What is a theme?
- Give an example of an event and a theme in a myth or legend you have read.
- What have you noticed about the characters in myths and legends?
- What have you noticed about the settings in myths and legends?

## Ideas for differentiation

**Support:** Organise these learners to work in a small adult-helper led group to produce a collaborative completed table.

**Extension:** Ask these learners to explore the types of themes used in other myths and legends they have read.

# Two Fast Runners

Once, a long time age, the antelope and the deer happened to meet on the prairie. They spoke together, giving each other the news, each telling what he had seen and done. After they had talked for a time the antelope told the deer how fast he could run, and the deer said that he could run fast too, and before long each began to say that he could run faster than the other. So they agreed that they would have a race to decide which could run the faster, and on this race they bet their galls. When they started, the antelope ran ahead of the deer from the very start and won the race and so took the deer's gall.

But the deer began to grumble and said, "Well, it is true that out here on the prairie you have beaten me, but this is not where I live. I only come out here once in a while to feed or to cross the prairie when I am going somewhere. It would be fairer if we had a race in the timber. That is my home, and there I can run faster than you. I am sure of it."

The antelope felt so glad and proud that he had beaten the deer in the race that he was sure that wherever they might run he could beat him, so he said, "Alright, I will run you a race in the timber. I have beaten you out here on the flat and I can beat you there." On this race they bet their dew-claws.

They started and ran this race through the thick timber, among the bushes, and over fallen logs, and this time the antelope ran slowly, for he was afraid of hitting himself against the trees or of falling over the logs. You see, he was not used to this kind of travelling. So the deer easily beat him and took his dew-claws.

Since that time the deer has had no gall and the antelope no dew-claws.

George Bird Grinnell

gall = gallbladder
timber = woods
dew-claw = small useless 'thumb'

*Cambridge Primary: Ready to Go Lessons for English Stage 3* © Hodder & Stoughton Ltd 2013

Name: _____

# Features of myths and legends

Use the table below to collect details from three myths or legends.

| Name of myth or legend | Characters | Setting | Events | Themes |
| --- | --- | --- | --- | --- |
|  |  |  |  |  |
|  |  |  |  |  |
|  |  |  |  |  |

# Character traits

### Learning objectives

- Write portraits of characters. (3Wf3)
- Identify pronouns and understand their function in a sentence. (3GPr4)
- Use question marks, exclamation marks, and commas in lists. (3GPw3)

### Resources

Photocopiable pages 69, 70, 76, 79 and 80; large pieces of paper; marker pens.

## Starter

- Place four large pieces of paper on tables around the classroom, each with one of the following headings: 'Appearance', 'Behaviour', 'Actions', 'Feelings'.
- Divide the learners into four groups and allocate each group to work on one of the pieces of paper.
- Tell the learners to think of a character they have met in a myth or legend and to write words or phrases under their heading that describe that aspect of the character, for example in 'Two Fast Runners' it says 'The antelope felt … **glad** and **proud**', so under the 'Feelings' heading the learners should write 'glad' and 'proud'.
- Make all the stories the learners have looked at available for reference. Rotate the learners around the room so that each group has an opportunity to make notes under each heading.

## Main activities

- Display an enlarged version of photocopiable page 79 and briefly explain what a 'Wanted' poster is. Explain that the learners will use one to collect and display information about a character.
- Recap on the term 'pronoun' and remind the learners how pronouns can be used to avoid repetition of the character's name.

- Hand out individual copies of photocopiable page 79 and tell the learners to pick a bad or evil character from one of the texts they have been reading for their 'Wanted' poster.
- Encourage them to use the vocabulary from the Starter activity to ensure they use the best words.
- Remind them to use correct punctuation for the poster, including question and exclamation marks for effect.

## Plenary

- Group the posters so that the same characters are together and let the learners view them in a table-top gallery. Ask the learners to focus on finding similarities and differences between the posters.
- Ask the learners to explain the features that the 'best' posters have and record these.

### Success criteria

Ask the learners:

- Give an example of how a character might be described in terms of their appearance, behaviour, actions and feelings.
- Where have you used question marks and exclamation marks on your poster? How do they help the reader?
- How might you use a pronoun?

### Ideas for differentiation

**Support:** Ask these learners to use photocopiable page 80 and draw and label a picture of their chosen character.

**Extension:** Ask these learners to consider their language choices to draw in the reader and make the poster as eye-catching as possible.

Name: _____

# Have you seen ...

Create a 'Wanted' poster for a bad or evil character from a myth or legend you have read. Remember to include plenty of information about the character:

- a picture and description of them
- what they are wanted for (the crime that has been committed)
- what the reward is (and who is paying it)
- any warnings (e.g. 'Do not approach!', 'Could be dangerous!')

WANTED

Name: _____

# Character portrait

Draw a picture of the main character from a myth or legend in the frame below. Add labels to your drawing that describe the character's:

- appearance
- actions
- behaviour
- feelings.

*Cambridge Primary: Ready to Go Lessons for English Stage 3* © Hodder & Stoughton Ltd 2013

# Storyboarding a myth or legend

## Learning objectives

- Plan main points as a structure for story writing. (3Wf5)
- Begin to organise writing in sections or paragraphs in extended stories. (3Wf6)
- Develop sensitivity to ways that others express meaning in their talk and non-verbal communication. (3SL8)

## Resources

Photocopiable pages 82 and 83; *Greek Myths* by Marcia Williams (Walker Books); internet access.

## Starter

- Display a page from *Greek Myths* by Marcia Williams (Walker Books), ensuring first that the content is suitable for your learners. Pages from her books can be found on the internet, for example at www.amazon.co.uk.
- Ask: *What is this way of telling a story called?* (Graphic novel, cartoon strip or storyboarding.) Discuss the combination of pictures, text and speech bubbles.
- Ask: *What do you think of this way of telling a story?*

## Main activities

- Explain to the learners that they are going to create a storyboard for a myth or legend of their choice, but they are going to plan the story out first and orally retell it before they start writing.
- Display an enlarged version of photocopiable page 82 and model filling in each box in turn using a myth or legend that the learners are familiar with. Ensure that they see how the structure of the story relates to each box.
- Distribute individual copies of photocopiable page 82 and ask the learners to fill in the basic story structure for a myth or legend of their choice.

- Next, tell the learners to check their plan by using it to tell their story to a partner. Ask them to make further notes on their planning frame, including any successful vocabulary they used or details of anything they forgot.
- Provide them with photocopiable page 83 and ask them to write their story as a storyboard using words and pictures, trying to capture any successful elements of their retelling.

## Plenary

- Ask each learner to put their storyboard out on their desk and then to go round the classroom looking at each other's storyboards.
- Ask the learners for examples of features they have seen that impressed them. Remind them that writing is personal and to be sensitive to the feelings of others.

## Success criteria

Ask the learners:

- How did you organise the events in your story?
- How did you decide which section to put each piece of information in?
- What is storyboarding? How is storyboarding different from how you normally write?
- What did you learn from watching others tell and perform their stories?

## Ideas for differentiation

**Support:** Organise these learners to work in a group, using the story plan that you created. Ask each learner to complete one or two storyboard frames on single pieces of paper and then join them together to create the whole storyboard.

**Extension:** Ask these learners to capture what the characters are saying using speech bubbles.

Name: _____

# Story structure

Use this writing frame to break down your chosen
story into its different parts.

**The introduction** – characters and setting

_____

_____

_____

**The problem** – how the story builds up

_____

_____

_____

**The main event** – what goes wrong, what needs sorting out

_____

_____

_____

**The resolution** – how the problem gets sorted out

_____

_____

_____

**The ending** – tying up the loose ends

_____

_____

_____

*Cambridge Primary: Ready to Go Lessons for English Stage 3* © Hodder & Stoughton Ltd 2013

Name: _____

# Storyboarding

Use this storyboarding frame to tell your story in words and pictures.

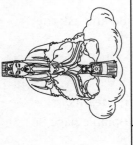

|  |  |  |  |  |  |  |  |
|---|---|---|---|---|---|---|---|
|  |  |  |  |  |  |  |  |
|  |  |  |  |  |  |  |  |

# Apostrophes and adverbs

## Learning objectives

● Recognise the use of the apostrophe to mark omission in shortened words, e.g. can't, don't. (3GPr2)

● Begin to vary sentence openings, e.g. with simple adverbs. (3GPw7)

## Resources

Photocopiable pages 69, 70, 76, 85 and 86; thick paper; glue; scissors; hat.

## Starter

• In advance, create a few sets of word cards from photocopiable page 85 using thick paper.

• Write 'he's', 'we're' and 'they're' on the board and ask the learners what the words mean.

• Explain the use of the apostrophe in these examples and discuss with the learners that this use of the apostrophe is a more casual way of speaking and writing.

• Organise the learners into small groups and give each group a set of word cards. Ask one learner in each group to take all the shaded cards and to share out the white cards between the other group members.

• Tell the first learner to turn over one shaded card and read it aloud to the group. Whoever has the corresponding white card receives the shaded one to make a pair. The winner is the first player to match up all their cards correctly.

## Main activities

• Ask the learners to identify the nouns, verb and adverb in the following sentence: 'Harry kicked the ball gently.'

• Ask: *What is an adverb?* Discuss the use of adverbs in our writing, for example to say how something is done, including how something is said.

• Distribute photocopiable pages 69 and 70 or 76 and ask the learners to work with a partner to spot adverbs in the text, drawing a line to link the adverb to its corresponding verb.

• Talk about how adverbs can also be used as sentence openers, for example: 'Quietly, it crept out of its dark hole.' Discuss how this technique can make our writing more interesting and exciting for the reader (as long as it is not overused).

• Distribute photocopiable page 86 and ask the learners to complete the activities.

## Plenary

• Divide the class into two or three teams.

• Cut out the adverbs on photocopiable page 86 and put them in a hat.

• Ask the learners to take it in turns to pick a word from the hat and mime the adverb to their team. How quickly can their team guess the adverb?

## Success criteria

Ask the learners:

● What is the job of the apostrophe in: 'I'm', 'they're' and 'we'd'?

● What does an adverb do?

● Why do writers use adverbs?

● Add an adverb as an opener to this sentence: 'She smiled at her grandma.'

## Ideas for differentiation

**Support:** Let these learners work with an adult helper who gives an oral choice of one correct and one incorrect adverb for the learners to choose from.

**Extension:** Challenge these learners to either write their own sentences or choose alternative adverbs from those on photocopiable page 86.

# Omission snap!

| | | | |
|---|---|---|---|
| he is | I will | she would | we are |
| I would | I am | they have | you would |
| she is | they will | he would | it is |
| I have | they would | you are | were not |

| | | | |
|---|---|---|---|
| he's | I'll | she'd | we're |
| I'd | I'm | they've | you'd |
| she's | they'll | he'd | it's |
| I've | they'd | you're | weren't |

# Opening sentences
# with adverbs

1. Use these adverbs as sentence openers to re-write the sentences below.

> firmly    noisily    quietly    loudly    greedily    quickly
>
> suddenly    nastily    tiredly    carefully    happily    badly
>
> slowly    gently    angrily    sweetly    sluggishly    awkwardly

a) Everyone feared the Bunyip.

_____

b) The girls passed the hole.

_____

c) The centipede appeared.

_____

d) Tyawan glided down to the forest floor.

_____

e) He searched and searched for his magic bone.

_____

f) The antelope ran ahead of the deer.

_____

2. Cross out the adverbs you have used in the box and write a new sentence using one of the adverbs that is left.

_____

_____

*Cambridge Primary: Ready to Go Lessons for English Stage 3* © Hodder & Stoughton Ltd 2013

# Planning a traditional story

## Learning objectives

- Plan main points as a structure for story writing. (3Wf5)
- Begin to adapt movement to create a character in drama. (3SL7)
- Adapt tone of voice, use of vocabulary and non-verbal features for different audiences. (3SL2)

## Resources

Photocopiable page 88; a favourite myth or legend.

## Starter

- Display an enlarged version of photocopiable page 88. Discuss with the learners how the path represents the story. Use a favourite myth or legend to model plotting the key events of the story along the path, alongside each advice box.
- Use both words and pictures.
- Divide the learners into five groups and allocate one section of the story to each group. Tell the learners they have five minutes to prepare to act out that scene, with different learners taking on the role of actors, directors, scenery, and so on.
- Let all the groups perform their scene in order.

## Main activities

- Distribute photocopiable page 88, if possible copied onto A3 paper, to the learners in pairs. Ask them to use the path to plan a new myth or legend, based heavily or lightly on a known myth or legend as they choose.
- Remind them that they are only writing a plan so they only need to write notes.
- Encourage them to stop frequently and tell or act out each part of the story to check they have included enough detail for the story to make sense. Model using the shared plan from the Starter activity to tell the story, using your voice to build up suspense and actions to make the story memorable.

- Ask the learners to practise telling their story a couple of times and then to share it with another pair.

## Plenary

- Ask: *What sort of actions did the good storytellers use?*
- Discuss any techniques mentioned, for example how the good storytellers took a brief pause to show the start of the next section or paragraph.
- Discuss what the learners have seen during the performances and give the learners an opportunity to amend and add to their plans as they reflect on this.

## Success criteria

Ask the learners:

- Explain the structure you have used to plan your story.
- What sort of actions did you use to help you tell your story?
- How can you use your voice to add suspense?
- What changes can you make to your plan after seeing another group's performance?

## Ideas for differentiation

**Support:** Ask these learners to focus on the first two sections of their plan and try to build up the suspense by using their voice.

**Extension:** Ask these learners to focus on how they can use their voice, actions and facial expressions to draw in the listeners by changing their tone and the pace they use.

Name: _____

# Planning frame for a myth or legend

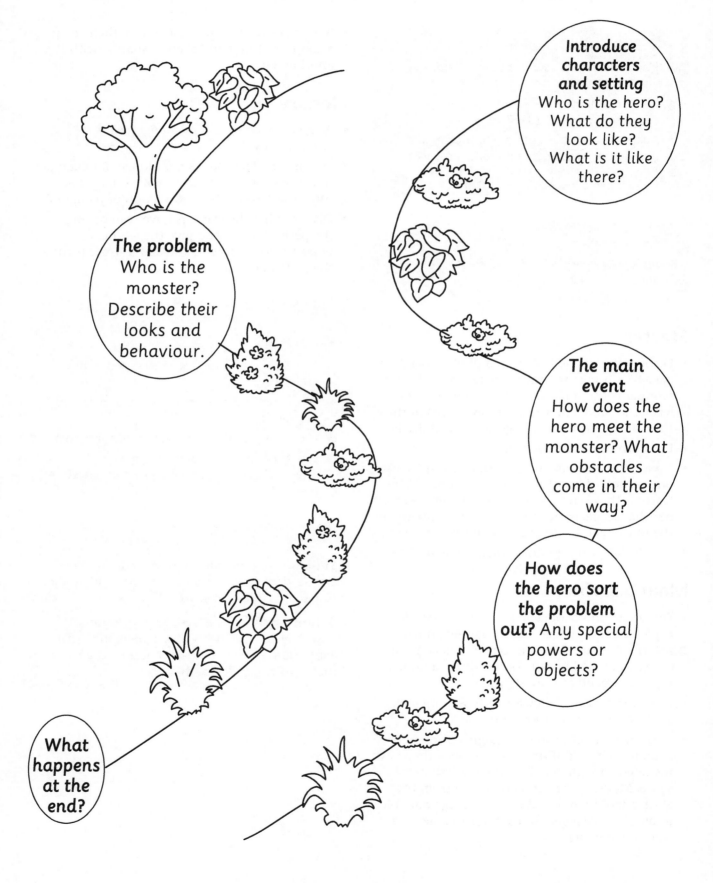

**Introduce characters and setting**
Who is the hero? What do they look like? What is it like there?

**The problem**
Who is the monster? Describe their looks and behaviour.

**The main event**
How does the hero meet the monster? What obstacles come in their way?

**How does the hero sort the problem out?** Any special powers or objects?

**What happens at the end?**

# Writing a traditional story

- Begin to organise writing in sections or paragraphs in extended stories. (3Wf6)
- Use a wider variety of sentence types including simple, compound and some complex sentences. (3GPw6)
- Develop range of adverbials to signal the relationship between events. (3Wf7)

Photocopiable pages 83, 88 (completed) and 90; scissors; writing books.

## Starter

- Write on the board: 'We couldn't go outside. There was a storm.'
- Ask the learners how we could change this into one sentence. (Add 'because'.)
- Discuss how two simple sentences joined together with a connective / conjunction make a compound sentence. Collect a list of as many connectives as the learners can think of.
- Organise the learners into pairs to play the Compound-sentences game on photocopiable page 90.
- Explain how we can use compound sentences and simple sentences together to make our writing more interesting to the reader, for example a series of short sentences is good to build up suspense. We couldn't go outside. There was a storm. Then suddenly a terrifying noise ...

## Main activities

- Display a completed version of photocopiable page 88 (from the previous lesson).
- Ask: *How can we use these sections to organise our writing?* (Each section will become a paragraph, possibly two paragraphs for the middle section of the story.)

- Display and model using a number of story and sentence openers to help the learners get started: 'Long, long ago ...', 'There was a time long ago ...', 'Before the world was very old, there lived a ...', 'A long time ago, before the world was very old ...', 'While she was waiting ...', 'Just as everything seemed to be going well ...', 'Then, as if by magic ...' and 'After a time ...'
- Ask the learners to return to the story plans they created with their partner and write a first draft of their own version of the story, using a new paragraph for each new section. Encourage them to share their thoughts with their partner as they go.

## Plenary

- Play 'Spot the connective'. This game will encourage the learners to use a greater range of connectives. Choose a confident learner to read through the first draft of their story. Ask the rest of the class to listen out for the connectives the learner has used and write them down. When the reader has finished, count up how many different connectives the learners heard.

Ask the learners:

- How can you make a compound sentence from two simple sentences?
- Should all your sentences have a connective?
- Tell me some of the adverbial connectives you have used today.
- How have you used your plan to write your first draft?

**Support:** Ask these learners to use photocopiable page 83 to storyboard their plan, picking out the key events.

**Extension:** Encourage these learners to explore their language choices to ensure they are using the best words to explain and describe to draw in the reader.

# Compound-sentences game

Cut out these simple sentences and connectives.
Re-arrange them to make compound sentences.

✂

| | | |
|---|---|---|
| The Bunyip was asleep. | She crept slowly past the cave. | |
| The noise echoed down the valley. | There was a snap as the twig broke. | |
| She ran all the way home. | She was safe this time. | |
| He leapt out and startled the monster. | He waited for the right moment. | |
| They were thankful it was all over. | They set off home. | |
| although | before | and | while | but | as | then | so |

# Editing and improving a traditional story

## Learning objectives

- Begin to organise writing in sections or paragraphs in extended stories. (3Wf6)
- Take turns in discussion, building on what others have said. (3SL3)
- Listen and respond appropriately to others' views and opinions. (3SL4)

## Resources

Photocopiable page 92; first draft of story from previous lesson.

## Starter

- Ask the learners to consider all the myths and legends they have been reading. Ask: *What stands out?* Collect as many ideas as possible.
- Tell the learners to work with a partner to decide what the success criteria might be for a good myth or legend. Ask: *What is the most important thing? Do you agree with your partner?*
- Ask each pair to join up with another pair to share their ideas and create a list that both pairs agree on.

## Main activities

- Tell each group of learners to appoint a spokesperson to present their ideas to the rest of the class.
- Collect the ideas from each group and display them. Put a tick by any duplicated ideas to show how many groups considered the point important.
- Display an enlarged version of photocopiable page 92 and read through the points together with the learners. Ask: *Do you agree with the list of success criteria?*
- Agree that providing the learners stick to the rules they decided upon then they will be successful in writing a myth or legend.

- Distribute photocopiable page 92 to the learners and instruct them to check their first draft against the criteria, then begin writing their final version, making changes as necessary.
- Interrupt the learners from time to time while they are writing to refocus them on the success criteria.

## Plenary

- Pair up each learner with a learner of a similar ability and tell each to read their partner's story.
- Encourage them to tick or leave blank the boxes against the success criteria.
- When the learners receive their story and success criteria back, give them an opportunity to make any corrections and alterations to their story.

## Success criteria

Ask the learners:

- How did you use paragraphs to organise your story?
- Why did it help to work with a partner to decide on the success criteria?
- Why have you used success criteria to check your writing?
- What changes did working with a partner help you to make?

## Ideas for differentiation

**Support:** Let these learners work in a small adult-helper led group to produce a collaborative story, with each learner writing a section or paragraph for the same story.

**Extension:** Ask these learners to include direct speech between the characters and extend the main event part of the story to provide exciting and interesting detail for the reader.

Name: _____

# Success criteria

Use this page to check your myth or legend.
Ask your partner to check it too.

| Success criteria | Author | Partner |
|---|---|---|
| I have written a story in paragraphs following my plan. | | |
| I have included a variety of sentence openers. | | |
| I have included a mixture of simple and compound sentences. | | |
| I have used full stops and capital letters. | | |
| I have written the story in the past tense. | | |
| I have described the character's looks, behaviour and feelings. | | |
| I have described the setting using my senses. | | |
| I have used these connectives: | | |

*Cambridge Primary: Ready to Go Lessons for English Stage 3* © Hodder & Stoughton Ltd 2013

# Unit assessment

- What can you tell me about myths and legends?
- What common themes do we often find in myths and legends?
- What similarities are there between the myths and legends you have been reading?

- What is the job of an adverb in a sentence? Give an example of an adverb.
- How do writers use adverbs in stories?
- What is a compound sentence?

## Summative assessment activities

Observe the learners while they play these games. You will quickly be able to identify those who appear to be confident and those who may need additional support.

### Mythical-character 'guess who?'

This activity helps to assess the learners' confidence in using adverbs.

**You will need:**

Photocopiable page 86; scissors; cards bearing the names of myth and legend creatures and characters the learners are familiar with; hat.

**What to do**

- Divide the class into mixed-ability teams of six to eight learners and give each team the list of adverbs from photocopiable page 86.
- Put the character cards in a hat and ask one learner to pick a card and share it with the rest of their team.
- In turn, each member of this team should now pick an adverb from the list and mime the character acting in this way.
- Challenge the other teams to guess who or what the character or creature is. If a team is successful, it is then their turn to choose a new character or creature.
- If there are no correct guesses, the team can give verbal clues about the character, for example where they live or what their favourite food is.

### Create a mythical creature

This activity helps to assess the learners' understanding of mythical creatures.

**You will need:**

Large pieces of paper; coloured pens.

**What to do**

- Explain to the learners that they are going to work in small groups of three or four to design a mythical creature.
- Display the list of features that the creature might have: a head (could be from another animal, could be more than one), body, arms, legs, wings, tail, skin, scales, fur, and so on.
- Ask the learners to draw the creature and annotate the drawing to include: the creature's personality, special powers or skills, and so on.
- Encourage the learners to link the creature's features with its skills or special powers, for example it has long legs – it can run faster than a cheetah.

- Distribute photocopiable page 94. (Ask the more-able learners to create their own design and layout.)
- Ask the learners to work independently to write a character profile for the mythical creature they have designed.
- Tell the learners to include:
  - a description of the creature's physical appearance
  - the creature's behaviour and character (dangerous, shy, and so on)
  - an explanation of any special power the creature has and when they use it.

Name: _____

# Character profile

Draw your mythical creature here and describe its features, behaviour, character and special powers.

**WANTED**

Description of _____

_____

_____

_____

_____

_____

_____

_____

Behaviour and character traits:

_____

_____

_____

_____

_____

_____

_____

Special powers:

_____

_____

_____

_____

_____

_____

_____

# Unit 2B: Letters

## Letters

- Identify the main purpose of a text. (3Rn6)
- Understand and use the terms 'fact', 'fiction' and 'non-fiction'. (3Rf8)
- Identify the main points or gist of a text. (3Rf6)

### Resources

Photocopiable pages 96 and 97; a large range of letters of different purposes: cards, postcards, envelopes, invitations, print-outs of emails.

## Starter

- Ask the learners to discuss these questions with a partner:
  - *What are letters?*
  - *Are they fact or fiction texts?*
  - *Who writes them?*
  - *What are they for?* (To communicate.)
  - *Do all letters come in envelopes?*
- Capture the learners' thoughts on the board.
- Ask: *Why do people send letters?* Ask the partners to spend two minutes drawing up a list of as many reasons as possible. (For friendship, to congratulate, to say 'thank you', and so on.)
- Share their lists and draw up a class list on the board.

## Main activities

- Distribute photocopiable page 96 and read the letters together with the learners. Ask: *What is the purpose of each letter?*
- Elicit the purpose of the letter from the specific language, for example: 'I am sorry.'
- Briefly discuss the apology letter. Ask: *What could this letter be mistaken for?* (The first line could confuse you into thinking it was a thank-you letter.)
- Ask: *What do you notice about the third letter?* (It is an email land is written in more casual language.)

- Distribute photocopiable page 97 and model finding evidence to fill in the first line.
- Provide the learners with access to a large range of letters, emails, postcards, invitations, and so on. Ask them to work in pairs to discuss the purpose of each letter, collecting evidence from the texts and filling in the table as they go along.

## Plenary

- Discuss how email could be used for most of the letters. Why do we still send postcards, letters, and so on?
- Ask: *How can we have a good idea about what a letter is about even before we read it?* (The layout of a postcard and the opening sentence give us clues.)

### Success criteria

Ask the learners:

- What are letters? Are they fiction or non-fiction?
- What kinds of letters are there?
- Explain the different types of layout for letters you have seen.
- What clues can you look for in a letter to tell you what it is about?
- What words and phrases would you expect to find in these letters: an invitation; a complaint; a recount?

### Ideas for differentiation

**Support:** Ask these learners to work in a group with an adult helper reading the letters on the photocopiable page and helping them to underline the vocabulary that explains the purpose of the letter.

**Extension:** Provide these learners with a range of more challenging letters to work on.

# Three letters

Dear Moo Cow's Milk Bar,

I am writing to let you know how angry I am about the new milkshake flavours you have put on your menu. What was wrong with strawberry and vanilla? Who ever heard of a pineapple and honey milkshake let alone guava and orange? Ridiculous! I want to know if these new flavours are some kind of joke or are they permanent? If they are permanent, I will be going elsewhere!

Yours furiously,

Maya Singh

Dear Ms Singh

Thank you very much for giving us your opinion of the new milkshake menu. I am so sorry you don't like the new flavours we are trying out here. We like to offer our  customers a wide choice, however in this case we have made a mistake. We have decided to go back to the classic flavours of strawberry, chocolate, vanilla and banana. We hope our loyal customers like you will soon return. Please bring this letter into the shop and receive a complimentary shake of your choice.

Kindest regards,

Moira Cowie

The owner of Moo Cow's Milk Bar

Hi there Kerena

I've heard back from my complaint letter to the owner of Moo Cow's and they are going back to the proper milkshake flavours! The best part is if I take her apology letter in with me I get a free milkshake to say sorry! I was thinking of going tomorrow at about 2p.m. – do you fancy coming with me?

Maya

Name: _____

# Reasons for writing a letter

| What is the purpose of the letter? | Which words tell us the purpose? | What is the format? (letter, card, email or postcard) |
|---|---|---|
| To complain | _____ _____ | _____ |
| To apologise | _____ _____ | _____ |
| To ask / find out something | _____ _____ | _____ |
| To celebrate or congratulate | _____ _____ | _____ |
| To invite | _____ _____ | _____ |
| To say thank you | _____ _____ | _____ |
| To recount / say what happened | _____ _____ | _____ |

# Features of a postcard

## Learning objectives

- Identify the main purpose of a text. (3Rn6)
- Consider ways that information is set out on page and on screen, e.g. lists, charts, bullet points. (3Rn4)
- Begin to infer meanings beyond the literal, e.g. about motives and character. (3Rf4)

## Resources

Photocopiable page 99; scissors; *Meerkat Mail* by Emily Gravett (MacMillan); a collection of postcards.

## Starter

- Hand round a range of postcards for the learners to look at.
- Briefly model reading one, for example: *Oh, it's from my sister. She's on holiday in Australia. This must be a picture of Perth.*
- To highlight the type of information that goes on a postcard, read it as if it were written in bullet points, for example:
  - *It's really warm and sunny.*
  - *She's stroked some baby kangaroos.*
  - *She's off on a 'learn to surf' course tomorrow!*

## Main activities

- Read *Meerkat Mail* by Emily Gravett to the learners. This picture book contains a series of postcards home from a travelling meerkat, with the classic features the learners should expect to find on a postcard. Discuss the different postcards in the book.
- Ask: *What features and information might we expect to find on a postcard?* Collect the learners' ideas, which might include:
  - written in the past tense (though with elements of present and future)
  - informal language
  - a comment on the weather
  - best thing about the place
  - what the writer has been doing, eating or seeing (recount)
  - usually lively, fun, upbeat and positive
  - what the accommodation is like
  - humorous pictures.

- Pass around the postcard used in the Starter and discuss the layout. Ask: *Where is the address? Where is the message? How much can the writer write?* Hand out Postcard 1 or Postcard 2 from photocopiable page 99 to each learner.
- Ask them to write a short recount on the postcard about an imagined holiday, including at least three brief pieces of information. Tell them to draw a picture of the holiday destination on the reverse.

## Plenary

- Ask the learners to put the finished postcards into a bag. Model dipping into the bag and pulling out a card and reading it. As you read, ask the learners to check it has the appropriate content and layout.
- Repeat with the learners working in pairs reading and content-checking.

## Success criteria

Ask the learners:

- Who sends postcards and why?
- What tense is a postcard written in?
- What three different sorts of information would you expect to find in this type of recount?
- Can you explain the layout of a postcard?

## Ideas for differentiation

**Support:** Provide these learners with Postcard 1 from photocopiable page 99.

**Extension:** Ask these learners to carry out some quick research about their chosen location using the internet.

# Writing postcards

Greetings from Dubai

## Postcard 1

Dear _____

The weather is _____

I've been to see _____

I'm really excited about tomorrow because we

are _____

The food has been _____

_____

Got to go – I'm off to _____

See you soon! _____

✂ — — — — — — — — — — — — — — — — — — — — — — — — — — — — — — — — — — —

## Postcard 2

Hi _____

The weather has been _____

I've _____

_____

Tomorrow we are _____

_____

_____

Got to go _____

_____

# Features of a letter

● Identify the main points or gist of a text. (3Rf6)

Photocopiable pages 101 and 102; multiple copies of thank-you letters, letters of apology, invitations and letters that recount something, such as postcards.

## Starter

- Display an enlarged version of photocopiable page 101, keeping the title hidden. Ask the learners what they think the writing frame could be used for. Discuss the distinctive layout used for writing letters.

- Ask the learners to explain the different sections. Point to the various sections and ask: *What goes here?* Model filling the different sections for a letter using the school address, the date and 'Dear Headteacher' and write an appropriate letter from the class.

- Ask the learners: *Why are letters set out in a similar way every time?* (Tradition, makes the different information easy to find.)

## Main activities

- Ask the learners to work in small groups and give each group a large selection of letters that fall into the following categories: thank-you letters, letters of apology, invitations and letters that recount something (such as postcards). Provide a mixture of handwritten and word-processed letters and different styles and subject matters if possible.

- Ask the learners to sort the letters into groups. The grouping could be by content or type of letter, the layout, word-processed or handwritten – whatever the learners decide.

- Ask them to explain their grouping criteria. Ask: *Why have you put these letters together?* Explain that it will be easier to compare letters of the same type and ask the learners to group the letters again by the type of letter, for example all the postcards together, if they've not done this already.

- Ask the groups to look at each letter type in turn and discuss the features that they can see across the different examples.

- Distribute individual copies of photocopiable page 102 and tell the learners, now working alone, to pick one of each type of letter and fill in information about its contents in the table.

## Plenary

- Ask: *What have you found out?* Encourage the learners to make statements like: 'All of the postcards have …', 'The address is always …'

- Discuss how the layout of a letter often helps identify the letter type before you read it, and if all letters follow this format it makes it quicker to skim and scan for information.

Ask the learners:

● Why do we set out letters in this way?
● Can you recognise different types of letter without reading them? How?
● How should an invitation close?
● What are the main differences between an invitation and a thank-you letter?

**Support:** Ask these learners to focus on two types of letter only: a thank-you letter and a postcard.

**Extension:** Ask these learners to focus on picking out the distinctive language of the different letter types.

Name: _____

# Letter-writing template

# Features of a letter

Complete the table for each type of letter.

| Feature | Thank-you letter | Letter of apology | Invitation | Recount letter or postcard |
|---|---|---|---|---|
| Language used | | | | |
| The type of opening used (Dear / To ….) | | | | |
| Type of closing used (From / Best wishes ….) | | | | |
| Where is the date? | | | | |
| What does the opening sentence tell you? | | | | |
| Where is the address of the person sending the letter written? | | | | |

*Cambridge Primary: Ready to Go Lessons for English Stage 3* © Hodder & Stoughton Ltd 2013

# Synonyms and shades of meaning

## Learning objectives

- Generate synonyms for high frequency words, e.g. big, little, good. (3PSV14)
- Use a dictionary or electronic means to find the spelling and meaning of words. (3PSV8)
- Consider words that make an impact, e.g. adjectives and powerful verbs. (3Rf7)

## Resources

Photocopiable pages 96 and 104; strips of paper and scissors; thesauruses and dictionaries.

## Starter

- Ask the learners: *What is a synonym?*
- Write on the board: 'The food was nice.' Ask the learners for words to replace 'nice'. (Delicious, mouth-watering, spectacular, amazing.) Discuss the slight change of meaning with each different word.
- Repeat the activity for: 'I got wet.' Ask the learners for words to replace 'wet'. (Drenched, soaked, sprayed.)
- Model using a thesaurus to find further synonyms for 'nice' and 'wet'.

## Main activities

- Agree that choosing the best word can really make a difference in sentences, and can help to draw the reader into the text.
- Ask: *How do we choose a word and make sure it's exactly what we mean?* Write 'yelled', 'whispered', 'thought' and 'snapped' onto different strips of paper and hand the strips out to four different learners. Tell the learners to organise themselves into a line from loudest to quietest. ('Yelled', 'snapped', 'whispered', 'thought'.) Let the rest of the class help advise them if necessary. When the order has been agreed, explain that this is known as shades of meaning – the meaning is similar but the strength of the word changes.

- Display an enlarged version of photocopiable page 96 and read the opening of the first letter. Ask: *What could the writer have said instead of 'angry'?*
- Distribute photocopiable page 104, dictionaries and thesauruses and ask the learners to carry out the activity.
- Provide the learners with four blank strips of paper and ask them to use their thesauruses to find one synonym each for 'big', 'small', 'hot' and 'cold' and write them on the strips.
- Challenge the class to work collaboratively to sort their strips into four displays, organising the words from strongest to weakest.

## Plenary

- Ask the learners to share what they have found with a partner, and then as a pair feed back to the rest of the class where they agreed and disagreed.
- Which words were tricky to order? Perhaps some were too similar?

## Success criteria

Ask the learners:

- 'Furious', 'cross', 'mad', 'annoyed', 'grumpy': Which is the strongest? Which is the weakest?
- What is 'shade of meaning'?
- How can synonyms help us with our writing?
- How can you use a dictionary or thesaurus to find a synonym for 'hungry'?

## Ideas for differentiation

**Support:** Ask these learners to do the same activity but without ranking the words in shades of meaning.

**Extension:** Ask these learners to make an additional collection of synonyms for 'excited'.

# Good and bad synonyms

1.  Cut out the words below and sort them into synonyms for 'good' and synonyms for 'bad'.

2.  Arrange each pile in order from strongest to weakest to show the shades of meaning.

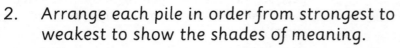

| good | super | unpleasant |
| terrible | excellent | wonderful |
| gruesome | splendid | nasty |
| horrible | ghastly | lovely |
| fantastic | great | dreadful |
| marvellous | awful | brilliant |
| outstanding | grim | magnificent |
| awesome | miserable | distressing |

*Cambridge Primary: Ready to Go Lessons for English Stage 3 © Hodder & Stoughton Ltd 2013*

# Thank-you letter

## Learning objectives

- Use and spell compound words. (3PSV2)
- Write letters, notes and messages. (3Wn3)
- Identify the main purpose of a text. (3Rn6)

## Resources

Photocopiable pages 101 and 106; scissors.

## Starter

- Write the following words on the board: 'everyone', 'somehow', 'anything', 'nowhere'.
- Ask the learners to read the words in pairs and look for any patterns.
- Discuss the term 'compound words'. Explain to the learners that it is important for them to recognise compound words as part of their strategy for recognising unfamiliar words when reading.
- Cut out the compound words on photocopiable page 106 and hand them out so that each learner has one word (using two copies of the page if necessary).
- Explain that the words are on either a shaded or a white background and challenge them to put a shaded and a white card together to create a compound word. (The words on the shaded background are the first half of the compound word.)
- Alternatively, give sets of the words to the learners in small groups to sort into a complete set of compound words.

## Main activities

- Briefly discuss why and when we write thank-you letters. *Has anyone ever written a thank-you letter? What did you say thank you for?*
- Distribute the bottom half of photocopiable page 106 and read it together with the learners. Discuss any unfamiliar vocabulary. Ask the learners to work with a partner to cut out and sort the pieces into the correct order.

- Explain to the learners that they are going to write a thank-you letter. Tell them it can be for something real or imaginary. Discuss possible ideas together. (To the kitchen staff for the lovely school dinners, to the fairy queen for your flying lessons, and so on).
- Distribute individual copies of photocopiable page 101 and ask the learners to use it to write their letter. Reiterate the layout of a letter.

## Plenary

- Ask the learners to share their thank-you letters in small groups.
- Discuss with the learners the sort of vocabulary you would expect to find in a good thank-you letter. Collect the learners' responses. (Friendly and personal, clearly saying what you are thankful for, a polite close, and so on.)

## Success criteria

Ask the learners:

- What is a compound word? Give me some examples.
- Explain the layout of a thank-you letter.
- What sort of ending might be used in a thank-you letter?
- What is the purpose of a thank-you letter?

## Ideas for differentiation

**Support:** Encourage these learners to follow the style and content ideas from photocopiable page 106.

**Extension:** Encourage these learners to be a bit more creative with the content of their letter by taking ideas and characters from books they have read.

# Thank-you letter

**Compound words**

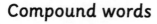

| | | | |
|---|---|---|---|
| news | paper | grand | mother |
| cup | board | rain | coat |
| gold | fish | bed | room |
| sun | shine | toe | nail |
| foot | ball | hair | brush |
| arm | pit | sheep | dog |
| eye | brow | tea | bag |
| dish | cloth | shoe | lace |
| post | box | play | time |

**Mixed-up letter**

| | |
|---|---|
| I also wanted to say a very big thank you for my fantastic gift. How did you know I collected elephants? It was very thoughtful of you and I love the expression on his face. He is now sitting at the desk with me watching me write this letter! | I hope we get the chance to meet up again before the summer as I didn't really get to talk to you about your new school and find out how you are getting on. |
| Kindest regards to you and your family, Asim | Dear Su, |
| 556 Sunny View Drive<br>Peterstown Village<br>Sunshine County<br>8 September 2013 | Thank you so much for coming to my party; I was really glad you could come. It was so good that so many of my friends and family could make it, and I felt very fortunate. |

*Cambridge Primary: Ready to Go Lessons for English Stage 3* © Hodder & Stoughton Ltd 2013

# Letter of complaint

- Scan a passage to find specific information and answer questions. (3Rn1)
- Begin to organise writing in sections or paragraphs in extended stories. (3Wf6)
- Collect examples of nouns, verbs and adjectives, and use the terms appropriately. (3GPr3)

## Resources

Photocopiable page 108; coloured pens, pencils or highlighters.

## Starter

- Display the words 'verb', 'noun' and 'adjective' on the board. Give the learners a few seconds to discuss with a partner what they mean.
- Distribute photocopiable page 108 and read the text together. Ask: *What can you tell me about the text?* (It is a complaint letter.)
- Provide the learners with three different coloured pens, pencils or highlighters. Ask them to locate the verbs, nouns and adjectives in the text and circle them in different colours.
- Ask the learners to work in small groups to check what they have done.

## Main activities

- Discuss the layout of the letter on photocopiable page 108. Ask the learners: *What can you tell me about it?*
- Get the learners to notice there are four paragraphs. Ask: *Why has it been written in sections?* Elicit from the learners that these sections are called paragraphs and that they are used to separate the information in the letter. Ask: *Why do writers use paragraphs?* (Change of time or place; change of character focus; change of action; or a new person speaking in dialogue.)

- Discuss the reasons why writers might use a new paragraph in a letter. (To organise ideas, to follow the correct layout of a letter, to show a change of theme or subject, to develop an idea.)
- Look again at photocopiable page 108 and together with the learners work out what each paragraph is about.
- When the learners are familiar with the letter and paragraphs, display these questions for them to answer:
  - 'Who is the letter to?'
  - 'Choose five words from the first paragraph that explain what the letter is about.'
  - 'What is the headteacher mainly concerned about?'
  - 'What is going to change that will make the problem worse?'
  - 'What are the possible options for a solution to the problem?'

## Plenary

- Give the learners an opportunity to discuss their answers with a partner.
- Split the learners into four groups and assign a paragraph to each group.
- Ask each group to scan the information in the paragraph and try to summarise their paragraph using as few words as possible.

## Success criteria

Ask the learners:

- What are paragraphs?
- How can we quickly recognise them?
- Why are they used in letters?
- What is a verb / noun / adjective? Give some examples.

## Ideas for differentiation

**Support:** Ask these learners to record the nouns, verbs and adjectives in a table.

**Extension:** Challenge these learners to look for synonyms to create a bank of verbs, nouns and adjectives.

# A letter to the police

MEADOW VIEW SCHOOL

Meadow View School
Paddock Road
Blaketown

10 September 2013

Police Headquarters
Hillside Street
Blaketown

Dear Chief Inspector Brown,

I am writing to complain that nothing has been done about the now extremely busy road outside my school. I have the safety of the children at my school to think about and this matter is causing me a great deal of worry. Something needs to be done to help the children cross the road safely.

Firstly, it is ridiculous that there is no safe pedestrian crossing outside my school or simply a police officer patrolling at busy times. I recognise that at the time the school was built Paddock Road was fairly quiet – there was a little bit of traffic in the mornings but it was easy enough for the children to cross the road. However, the road has got much busier in recent years and the cars are getting faster. There have been many new houses built so more people have moved to this area and more children now come to our school. The road is very dangerous.

In addition, Paddock Road is going to get even busier in the next year as the new supermarket opens. I want to know what you are going to do to ensure the safety of my children as they cross the road to come to school.

I trust that you will give this matter your full attention in order to sort out the problem of the fast cars and no safe place for children to cross to get to school.

Yours sincerely,
Mr C. Troll
Headteacher

# Plurals

## Learning objectives

- Understand pluralisation and use the terms 'singular' and 'plural'. (3GPr6)
- Use a dictionary or electronic means to find the spelling and meaning of words. (3PSV8)
- Make a record of information drawn from a text, e.g. by completing a chart. (3Wn4)

## Resources

Photocopiable pages 110 and 111; the learners' reading books.

## Starter

- Display the words 'singular', 'plural' and 'pluralisation' on the board. Ask: *What do they mean?* Collect possible ideas from the learners. Ask: *How can we be sure of the meaning?* (Check in a dictionary.)
- Ask the learners to discuss with a partner and come up with the singular and plural for a range of words: 'leaf', 'rabbit', 'teachers', and so on.
- Write the discussed words and plurals on the board and point out the different ways the root word changes. Ask: *How do we know which is the correct spelling?*

## Main activities

- Tell the learners that they are going to investigate singular and plural words to find some rules to use to help them spell them correctly.
- Distribute photocopiable page 110. Ask the learners to look through their reading books and write any plurals they find there in the correct box on the photocopiable page for how it is spelt, and add the singular to the first column.

- Display an enlarged version of the following rules:
  - For most words: add **-s** (so 'cat' becomes 'cats')
  - Words ending in **s**, **sh** or **ch**: add **-es** (so 'church' becomes 'churches')
  - Words ending in **f** (or **fe**): remove the **f** (or **fe**) and add **-ves** (so 'leaf' becomes 'leaves')
  - Words ending in a consonant followed by **y**: remove the **y** and add **-ies** (so 'library' becomes 'libraries')
  - Words ending in a vowel then **y**: simply add **-s** (so 'monkey' becomes 'monkeys').
- Go through these rules one at a time and ask the learners for examples from their table.
- Hand out individual copies of photocopiable page 111 and ask the learners to correct the mistakes.

## Plenary

- Ask the learners to discuss with a partner any words that completely change in the plural, for example: 'person', 'mouse', 'child', 'man', 'goose', 'foot', 'woman', 'tooth'; or stay exactly the same, for example: 'sheep', 'deer'. Ask: *Can you think of any others?*
- Discuss how there are many exceptions to spelling rules in English.

## Success criteria

Ask the learners:

- Explain the rule for adding '-ies' to make a plural.
- When do you add '-es' to make a plural?
- How can you check the spelling of a plural?

## Ideas for differentiation

**Support:** Ask these learners to focus on plurals that add 's'.

**Extension:** Ask these learners to explore plurals where the word changes completely (person / people) or stays the same (sheep / deer).

# Singular and plural investigation

Use this table to find out how to spell different plurals.
Two have been done for you.

| Singular | Plural: add '-s' | Plural: add '-es' | Plural: add '-ves' | Plural: add '-ies' | Plural: change word |
|---|---|---|---|---|---|
| cat | cats | | | | |
| child | | | | | children |
| | | | | | |
| | | | | | |
| | | | | | |
| | | | | | |
| | | | | | |
| | | | | | |

Name: _____

# Postcard plurals

Read this postcard carefully. Cross out the wrong spellings for the plurals.

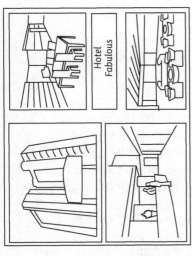

Hotel Fabulous

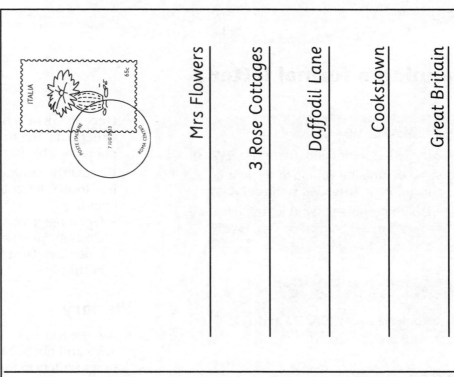

ITALIA

POSTE ITALIANE  7 IUG 2013  ROMA CENTRO

65c

Mrs Flowers

3 Rose Cottages

Daffodil Lane

Cookstown

Great Britain

Hi Grandma

We're on our holidayes / holidays in Italy and having a great time.
Wish you were here too! The placies / places we have been staying
in are amazing. Some of the hotelies / hotels are really posh. One
had a man who parks the cars/cares for you and every room has
fresh flowers / floweres in it! We're going for lots of walks / walkes
to see the sights / sightes and later Mum said we could go to one of
the beaches / beachies and get ice lollyes / lollies to cool us all
down!

Bye for now,

Jayden

PS. Staying up late tonight to see some fireworks / fireworkes.

# Planning a formal letter

- Write letters, notes and messages. (3Wn3)
- Begin to organise writing in sections or paragraphs in extended stories. (3Wf6)
- Establish purpose for writing, using features and style based on model texts. (3Wn2)

**Resources**

Photocopiable pages 108, 113 and 114.

## Starter

- Display an enlarged version of photocopiable page 108 and read it aloud. Ask: *Is this a good letter? Is the message clear? What would we expect to see or read in a good letter?*
- Discuss how the letter is addressing an issue affecting a school and the children who go to that school. Either choose or let the learners choose an issue that affects them – changes to the playground, school lunches, a busy road near the school, and so on.
- Spend some time discussing the issue as a class, then encourage the learners to explore the details of the issue in small groups. Ask them to make notes about the problem, who the letter should be addressed to, the reason for writing, how the problem affects the learners and a possible solution to resolve it.

## Main activities

- Discuss possible success criteria and display an enlarged copy of photocopiable page 114. Discuss further criteria: *Does the letter make sense? How could it be improved? Have you used the best words to explain and describe? Anything else?*
- Ask the learners to work in pairs and use photocopiable page 113 to plan the letter, keeping in mind the success criteria.

- Once the plan is finished, the learners can either write the first draft on a new copy of photocopiable page 113 or on lined paper.
- Discuss the closing of the letter. Explain how in a formal letter the closing depends on the opening:
  - Opening: 'Dear [the name of the person]'; closing: 'Yours sincerely'
  - Opening: 'Dear Sir / Madam'; closing: 'Yours faithfully'.

## Plenary

- Ask the learners to share some of their key ideas and notes. Model turning these into fuller sentences for them, for example: 'small playground' becomes 'I am outraged at the size of the field a whole school is expected to play on – there is not nearly enough space.'
- When the learners have heard each other's ideas, give them an opportunity to make notes and changes to improve their first draft.

**Success criteria**

Ask the learners:

- How would you lay out a formal letter?
- Why do we use these strict rules for formal letters?
- What features would you expect to find in a formal letter?
- How are formal letters different from emails and letters we send to our friends and family?

**Ideas for differentiation**

**Support:** Help these learners to plan the paragraphs for their letter and provide them with suitable vocabulary.

**Extension:** Encourage these learners to consider their choice of language to best explain their issue and outline a possible solution to the problem.

Name: _____

# Writing frame for a formal letter

_____
_____
_____
_____

_____
_____
_____
_____

Dear Sir / Madam,

I am writing _____
_____
_____

Firstly, _____
_____
_____

In addition, _____
_____
_____

I trust that you will give this matter your full attention in order to sort out

the problem of the _____

Yours faithfully,

_____

Name: _____

# Formal letter success criteria

Use this page to check your letter. Ask your partner to check it too.

| Success criteria | Author | Partner |
|---|---|---|
| The sender's address is at the top right. | | |
| The date is under the sender's address at the right. | | |
| The address of the person the letter is to is at the left side. | | |
| The letter starts: 'Dear Sir / Madam' or 'Dear Mr / Mrs / Miss …' | | |
| There are paragraphs to explain the reason for writing. | | |
| The letter clearly says what the sender would like. | | |
| The letter is written in paragraphs with a line left between paragraphs. | | |
| Full stops and capital letters are correctly used. | | |
| The letter uses an appropriate sign-off line ('faithfully' if the letter is addressed 'Dear Sir / Madam' or 'sincerely' if it is addressed to 'Mr / Mrs / Miss …'). | | |

*Cambridge Primary: Ready to Go Lessons for English Stage 3* © Hodder & Stoughton Ltd 2013

# Editing and improving a letter

## Learning objectives

- Write letters, notes and messages. (3Wn3)
- Begin to organise writing in sections or paragraphs in extended stories. (3Wf6)
- Establish purpose for writing, using features and style based on model texts. (3Wn2)

## Resources

Photocopiable pages 113 (completed), 114 and 116.

## Starter

- Display an enlarged copy of photocopiable page 116. Ask the learners to discuss what they think of the letter with a partner.
- Distribute photocopiable pages 114 and 116 and ask the learners to use the success criteria to establish the problems.

## Main activities

- Confirm with the learners that the main issue with the letter is that there is not enough information or detail. The writer is clearly very angry but has not stated the issues in a clear, ordered way.
- Establish that it should end 'Yours faithfully'.
- On an enlarged copy of photocopiable page 116, model using the learners' ideas and the success criteria to improve the letter using the space provided, for example add a brief introduction such as: 'I am a regular customer in [shop name]'. Also add structured and specific points: 'On a recent visit there were rotten vegetables on the floor …', 'After being a customer for so many years I am extremely disappointed …', 'I will be calling in again next week when I will discuss the matter with you and hope to see an improvement', and so on.

- Ask the learners to reflect on this work by reading the first draft of their letter (completed in the last lesson) with fresh eyes. Ask: *Are you making your point clearly?*
- Tell the learners to use their first draft by reading it through several times then checking it against the success criteria on photocopiable page 114.
- Ask them to work with a partner, read each other's letters and mark them against the success criteria.

## Plenary

- Give some of the learners an opportunity to share their letters with the rest of the class.
- Post as many of the letters as possible. Ask: *How would we feel if no one replies to the letter?* (Disappointed?) Reiterate how important it is to reply to a letter.

## Success criteria

Ask the learners:

- What features make a letter a formal letter?
- How have you used paragraphs to organise your writing?
- Why is it important to make your point clearly in a letter?
- How do you know whether to use 'Yours faithfully' or 'Yours sincerely'?

## Ideas for differentiation

**Support:** Organise these learners to work in a small adult-helper led group and compose a group letter.

**Extension:** Expect these learners to write a letter to a real person regarding a real issue.

Name: _____

# What's missing?

There are a lot of problems with this letter.
Can you help to make it better?

Dear Sir / Madam,

I am writing to let you know how furious I am about what I have just seen!

_____

_____

_____

_____

The mess was absolutely disgraceful; I have never seen such a sight

in all my life. Your company should be ashamed of yourselves.

_____

_____

_____

_____

I would like this problem sorted out as soon as possible, otherwise I will be contacting the environmental health organisation, who will take further action.

_____

_____

_____

_____

Yours sincerely

Mrs Veronica Angry

*Cambridge Primary: Ready to Go Lessons for English Stage 3* © Hodder & Stoughton Ltd 2013

# Unit assessment

- What kinds of letters can you tell me about?
- Explain the different kinds of layout you might find in a postcard / a letter to a friend / a formal letter?
- What are the differences between a thank-you letter and a formal letter?

- Which are best, emails or letters?
- How would you close a letter?
- What is a compound word? Give some examples.

## Summative assessment activities

Observe the learners while they play these games. You will quickly be able to identify those who appear to be confident and those who may need additional support.

### Synonym race

This game helps the learners to think about using a wider variety of vocabulary.

**You will need:**

One piece of paper per pair; a stopwatch; a bell; dictionaries and thesauruses.

**What to do**

- Pair up the learners and give each pair a piece of paper.
- Tell the learners to fold their paper into four and write one of the following words as a heading in each quarter: 'big', 'small', 'hot' and 'cold'.
- Give the learners one minute to write on the paper as many synonyms for 'big' as they can. Ring a bell and then give them another minute for each of the other words in turn, ringing a bell whenever they should switch words.
- Ask the learners to swap papers with another pair and provide dictionaries and thesauruses for them to mark how many of the words are correct.
- The winning team will be the one with the most words. There will be four winners: one for each section. In the case of a tie-break the number of correct spellings will decide!

### Plurals match

This activity gives the learners an opportunity to practise recognising how spelling is altered from singular to plural.

**You will need:**

Photocopiable page 118; scissors; dice; dictionaries.

**What to do**

- Create word cards from photocopiable page 118. Ask the learners to work in groups of three or four and give each group a set of the cards, the key from photocopiable page 118 and a dice.
- Tell the learners to take four cards each and place them face up in front of them. The remaining cards should be placed in a pile in the middle.
- Tell the learners to take it in turns to roll the dice. If they have a word that is made into a plural by adding whatever the dice says (see the key), they should turn over the card (the rest of the learners can check, using a dictionary if necessary), for example if a card has 'baby' written on it and the learner rolls a 4, they get to turn it over as the plural of 'baby' is 'babies'.
- The winner is the first to turn over all their cards. The game can be repeated by shuffling the cards and starting again.

Ask the learners to work independently and to use what they have learnt about letters of recount to make and write a postcard to a friend about something they have done recently.

# Plural match

| | | | | |
|---|---|---|---|---|
| city | monkey | tooth | fox | loaf |
| witch | person | toy | desk | sheep |
| dish | brush | window | wolf | tune |
| party | jelly | donkey | child | mouse |
| kitten | berry | leaf | day | tick |
| baby | goose | calf | puppy | shoe |

**Key**

1 – add '-s'    2 – add '-es'    3 – add '-ves'    4 – add '-ies'

5 – change word    6 – do not change word

# Unit 2C:  Poems from different cultures

## Reading and sharing poems

## Starter

- Distribute individual copies of photocopiable page 120 and copies of poems from around the world (for example from www.poetrylibrary.edu. au/poems-theme-occasion/poems-for-kids).
- Explain that the poems come from different parts of the world and from different cultures. Ask: *What does this mean?*
- Read a selection of the poems out loud.
- Ask the learners if they can see any clues from within the poems themselves as to where they might have come from, for example any place names, animals in the poems or the language used in descriptions, and so on. Discuss these together.

## Main activities

- Ask the learners to work in small groups and ask the groups to read the poems aloud to each other and discuss any clues as to where the poems have come from.
- Ask: *Could the poems have been written in this country?* Ask the learners to justify their ideas from the text.
- Distribute three copies of photocopiable page 121 to each learner and display an enlarged version.
- Ask the learners to use the frame to organise their ideas about three of the poems they have been reading, remembering their group discussions.

- Model filling in the frame for one of the shared poems, for example for 'Classes under the trees' under the heading 'Effects' you might write: '"Children, we can't breathe in here" – This makes me think of when it's really hot and we're inside and the air is still and heavy. I know exactly what she means!'
- Discuss a few other ideas from the learners about their likes and dislikes.
- Encourage them to reference the text to support or back up their ideas with examples.

## Plenary

- Give the learners an opportunity to reflect on their and others' responses.
- Organise the learners to work with a partner who has looked at at least one of the same poems. (This needs to be someone they were not working with in the group activity.)
- Tell the learners to look at each other's responses to the same poem and to look for two similarities and two differences in their opinions.

# Poems from different cultures

## Classes Under the Trees

My teacher, Mrs Zettie, says,
'Children, we can't breathe in here.
Come on! We're going
under the breadfruit tree!'

We leave the one room schoolhouse
these hot days in June
for the breeze outdoors
below blue skies.

Reciting our lessons
in singsong fashion,
we hear twittering birds
recite theirs, too.

Monica Gunning
(Jamaican)

## Red

Red is the colour
of my Blood;
of the earth,
of which I am a part;
of the sun as it rises, or sets,
of which I am a part;
of the blood
of the animals,
of which I am a part;
of the flowers, like the waratah,
of the twining pea,
of which I am a part;
of the blood of the tree
of which I am a part.
For all things are a part of me,
and I am a part of them.

W. Les Russell
(Australian Aborigine)
waratah = a red flower

Name: _____

# Poetry response

Use this frame to collect your thoughts and feelings about a poem you have read.

**Name of poem:**
_____

**Personal response**

What do you like or dislike about the poem?

_____

_____

_____

_____

_____

**Pictures**

What pictures does the poem paint in your mind? Why does this happen?

_____

_____

_____

_____

**Effects**

How does the poem make you feel?

_____

_____

_____

_____

_____

# Patterns in poems

## Learning objectives

- Read a range of story, poetry and information books and begin to make links between them. (3Rf9)
- Consider how choice of words can heighten meaning. (3PSV11)
- Practise learning and reciting poems. (3Rf12)

## Resources

Photocopiable pages 123 and 124; coloured pens.

## Starter

- Display an enlarged version of photocopiable page 123 and read the poem with the learners.
- Underline the rhyming words in the first verse with coloured marker pens, using different colours for different rhymes, for example: 'town', 'brown' and 'down' in one colour and 'shiver' and 'river' in another.
- Repeat for the next verse, underlining 'bends', 'friends' and 'descends' in one colour and 'elusive' and 'exclusive' in another.
- Elicit from the learners that a pattern is emerging. (Lines 1, 3 and 4 rhyme and lines 2 and 5 rhyme.)
- Distribute individual copies of photocopiable page 123 and coloured pens and tell the learners to continue underlining the rhyming patterns to the end of the poem.

## Main activities

- Distribute photocopiable page 124 and tell the learners to look for a pattern in this poem, highlighting the rhymes as before.
- Discuss how patterns in poems often make them easier to read and learn by heart.
- As a class, learn one of the poems by heart. Read the chosen poem through with the learners at a pace that they will be able to match, modelling how to use the commas and full stops as clues as to when to breathe and pause.

- If the class is learning 'Old Man Platypus', they could work in teams with each team taking a verse to recite together, choral style. When they're confident with their verse, they can try a second verse, and so on.
- Once the learners begin to get confident with the whole poem, give them some time to practise as a class, keeping in time with each other. Remind them that it's not a race!

## Plenary

- Provide the learners with an opportunity to perform their rehearsed and possibly memorised poem in groups or individually, depending on their confidence.
- Ask the learners:
  - Which lines were easiest to remember?
  - Where there any tricky phrases to 'get your tongue around'?
- Discuss how enjoyable it is to share poetry in this way – poems come alive when they are performed!

## Success criteria

Ask the learners:

- Explain a pattern have you found in a poem.
- What patterns have you seen in poems?
- What effect does the pattern have on the poem?
- How can a rhyming pattern help you to learn to recite a poem?

## Ideas for differentiation

**Support:** Give these learners a line each to learn to perform.

**Extension:** Challenge these learners to add actions and use their voices to create different effects in reading the poems.

# Old Man Platypus

Far from the trouble and toil of town,
Where the reed beds sweep and shiver,
Look at a fragment of velvet brown —
Old Man Platypus drifting down,
Drifting along the river.

And he plays and dives in the river bends
In a style that is most elusive;
With few relations and fewer friends,
For Old Man Platypus descends
From a family most exclusive.

He shares his burrow beneath the bank
With his wife and his son and daughter
At the roots of the reeds and the grasses rank;
And the bubbles show where our hero sank
To its entrance under water.

Safe in their burrow below the falls
They live in a world of wonder,
Where no one visits and no one calls,
They sleep like little brown billiard balls
With their beaks tucked neatly under.

And he talks in a deep unfriendly growl
As he goes on his journey lonely;
For he's no relation to fish nor fowl,
Nor to bird nor beast, nor to horned owl;
In fact, he's the one and only!

'Banjo' Paterson

# My Sari

Saris hang on the washing line:

a rainbow in our neighbourhood.

This little orange one is mine,

it has a mango leaf design.

I wear it as a Rani would.

It wraps around me like sunshine,

it ripples silky down my spine,

and I stand tall and feel so good.

Debjani Chatterjee

Rani = a queen

# Comparing stories and poems

### Learning objectives

● Read a range of story, poetry and information books and begin to make links between them. (3Rf9)

● Identify the main purpose of a text. (3Rn6)

### Resources

A range of picture books the learners are familiar with; a range of poems or poetry anthologies; photocopiable page 126; scissors.

## Starter

• Spend some time reading a few opening pages of a few different picture books, preferably ones the learners are somewhat familiar with.

• Repeat this with the opening lines of some poems.

• Elicit from the learners that there are some clear differences between books and stories and poems.

## Main activities

• Cut out an enlarged version of the cards on photocopiable page 126 and distribute them amongst the learners. Spend some time reading and explaining, where necessary, what they all mean.

• Ask the learners to work in pairs and give each pair a story picture book and a poem or poetry anthology.

• Ask them to examine and discuss the features of the story they have and the features of the poems. Ask them to read their cards one at a time and look for an example of each statement in either the book or a poem.

• Next ask them to divide the cards into two piles: 'statements about stories' and 'statements about poems'. Explain that if they think a card describes both genres, they have to decide which it fits better.

• While the learners are working, move between the pairs to discuss any unusual examples.

• Once they have completed the task, collectively come up with the 'best example' for each card from the texts the learners have read, and organise them into a display for the learners to reflect on.

## Plenary

• Tell the learners to compare their two piles of cards with at least two other pairs.

• Ask: *Were there any that could go in both piles? Did you all agree?* (Picture books are often written like a poem.)

• Ask the learners to discuss if they found any features that did not have a card.

• Encourage them to provide examples of any texts that were confusing as they contained examples of both features of poems and stories. Explain the term 'narrative poem' (a poem that tells a story).

### Success criteria

Ask the learners:

● What are the differences between stories and poems?

● What features would you expect to find in a poem?

● What features would you expect to find in a story?

● What can you tell me about poems that tell a story?

### Ideas for differentiation

**Support:** Ask these learners to work in a small adult-helper led group and put sticky notes on the texts to identify their examples.

**Extension:** Ask these learners to look for examples of narrative poems using online poetry anthologies.

# Poems and stories

Cut out and sort these statements about poems and stories.

They can have a rhythm or beat when you read them.

They are divided into paragraphs and chapters.

They sometimes have rhyming words.

Sometimes they are divided into verses.

The words can make a shape on the page.

The words can make a pattern on the page.

They tend to be short.

Some can be thousands of words long, over hundreds of pages.

They are written left to right, making a rectangle shape on the page.

*Cambridge Primary: Ready to Go Lessons for English Stage 3* © Hodder & Stoughton Ltd 2013

# Themes in poems

## Learning objectives

● Read a range of story, poetry and information books and begin to make links between them. (3Rf9)

● Identify different types of stories and typical story themes. (3Rf5)

● Make a record of information drawn from a text, e.g. by completing a chart. (3Wn4)

## Resources

Dictionaries; photocopiable page 128; a number of poetry anthologies.

## Starter

• Discuss the term 'theme' with the learners. Ask: *What is a theme?* Tell them to discuss the term with a partner and then to look it up in a dictionary and discuss the dictionary definition.

• Explain that a theme is the overall idea that the poem is about, for example: 'Family', 'The seasons', 'Childhood' or 'School'. Ask: *Can you think of any other themes you've come across or that you would be interested in writing about?*

• Display the list of possible themes the learners come up with for them to refer back to when they are doing the Main activity.

## Main activities

• Distribute photocopiable page 128 and read through the headings with the learners to check their understanding.

• Provide the learners with access to a wide variety of poems or poetry anthologies and ask them to work with a partner.

• Ask the partners to search through the poems to find one they would like to write about. Tell them to take time to read the poem carefully together and then to discuss what the possible themes are and what they think about the poem. Explain that they don't need to agree what the themes are or what they think about the poem. Explain that you want their personal response to the poems, so no answer will be right or wrong.

• Ask the learners to fill in the first line of the table and then choose another poem.

## Plenary

• Share examples of poems the learners found with more than one theme.

• Ask: *How does the theme of the poem affect how we might feel about it?* (Possibly empathy, enjoyment, excitement, laughter, and so on.)

• Give each pair the opportunity to share a poem they have found. Tell the audience to listen out for what they think the theme is and then see if they agree with the pair who found it.

## Success criteria

Ask the learners:

● What is a theme?

● How do poets use themes in their poems?

● Give examples of some of the themes you have seen in the poems you have read.

● What effect can the theme have on the person reading the poem?

## Ideas for differentiation

**Support:** Ask these learners to do the Main activity with one of the poems they are familiar with.

**Extension:** Encourage these learners to look at poems that are not familiar to them.

Name: _____

# Spot the theme

Use this table to collect your thoughts about the themes you have found in poems.

| Name of poem | Main theme | Additional themes and how we feel about the poem |
|---|---|---|
|  |  |  |
|  |  |  |
|  |  |  |
|  |  |  |
|  |  |  |
|  |  |  |
|  |  |  |
|  |  |  |

# Poetic devices

### Learning objectives

● Explore words that have the same spelling but different meanings (homonyms), e.g. form, wave. (3PSV7)

● Consider how choice of words can heighten meaning. (3PSV11)

### Resources

Photocopiable pages 130 and 131; dictionaries.

## Starter

- Briefly discuss the term 'poetic devices' and elicit from the learners that these are techniques used by poets to create effects, for example to emphasise a word or emotion.

- Introduce the learners to the term 'homonym' (words with the same spelling but different meanings).

- Display an enlarged version of photocopiable page 130 and read it together with the learners.

- Give some examples of words that are spelt the same but have two or more meanings, modelling how to use the dictionary to check the meanings.

- Demonstrate filling in the table with two different sentences that show the different meanings.

- Distribute photocopiable page 130 to the learners and ask them to complete it individually or with a partner. Provide dictionaries to help them complete the task.

## Main activities

- Ask the learners what they know about any other poetic devices, for example:
  - rhyme
  - alliteration (a repeated sound)
  - onomatopoeia (a word that forms a sound when it is said, for example 'sizzle', 'bang', and so on)
  - simile (a comparison, for example 'as cool as a cucumber')
  - metaphor (something described as something else, for example 'she had eyes of moonlight').

- Explain to the learners that they will explore similes and metaphors in this lesson. Spend some time discussing and explaining the differences:
  - A metaphor says something **is** something else: 'He **is** a tower of strength'.
  - A simile **compares** one thing to another: 'He is **as** strong **as** an ox'.

- Ask the learners to give you examples of each.

- Distribute photocopiable page 131 and ask the learners to complete the page with a partner.

## Plenary

- Organise the learners into groups of four to six and ask them to create similes to describe a:
  - tree
  - building
  - wild animal.

- See how many metaphors they can create for the Sun (for example: 'The Sun is a lake of fire').

- Give the learners an opportunity to feed back their ideas and create a display for future reference.

### Success criteria

Ask the learners:

● What are poetic devices? Why do poets use them?

● What effects can they have on the poem and the reader?

● Give an example of a simile and a metaphor.

● What is a homonym? Give an example.

### Ideas for differentiation

**Support:** Ask these learners to work with a partner for the Starter activity to create the two sentences.

**Extension:** Ask these learners to use some poetry anthologies to search for other examples of similes and metaphors and discuss how they improve the poem.

Name: _____

# Same word – different meaning

Show two different meanings for these homonyms.
Some have been done for you.

| Example of meaning 1 | Word | Example of meaning 2 |
|---|---|---|
| Don't skip a chapter or the book won't make sense. | skip | You can either skip, hop or jump in the race. |
| | miss | |
| | draw | Neither team won. It was a draw. |
| | Bill | |
| | kid | |
| | left | |
| | May | Please may I leave the table? |
| | nail | |
| | fine | |
| | match | |
| I caught a cold and couldn't stop sneezing. | cold | |
| | glasses | |
| | ball | |
| | mark | |

*Cambridge Primary: Ready to Go Lessons for English Stage 3* © Hodder & Stoughton Ltd 2013

Name: _____

# Poetic devices

1.  Use these phrases to help you write three similes.

| as brave as | as tall as | as bright as |
|---|---|---|
| eyes like | with fur as soft as | he had legs like |
| as slow as | as busy as | with teeth like |

a) _____

b) _____

c) _____

2.  Draw a line to match the metaphor with its meaning.

| | |
|---|---|
| Hold your tongue. | To annoy or irritate someone. |
| I have heavy eyes. | Feeling sad. |
| To rub someone up the wrong way. | Things are going to be good. |
| Let the cat out of the bag. | I'm feeling sleepy. |
| Down in the mouth. | Keep quiet. |
| The future looks bright. | Give away a secret. |

3.  Write two more metaphors of your own.

a) _____

b) _____

# Writing poems

## Learning objectives

- Consider how choice of words can heighten meaning. (3PSV11)
- Ensure grammatical agreement of pronouns and verbs in using standard English. (3GPw5)
- Write and perform poems, attending to the sound of words. (3Wf9)

## Resources

Photocopiable page 133.

## Starter

- Tell the learners that in this lesson they are going write a short poem. The theme of animals works well for children's poems, but this lesson could easily be adapted for another theme.

- Act out and describe a number of animals and ask the learners to guess what they are, for example stand on tip-toes and make long shapes with your arms and legs, then say: *I am strong and I have legs as tall as a skyscraper. What am I?*

- Ask the learners to act out and describe some animals for a partner to guess.

- Encourage them to use what they know about poetic devices to make their descriptions as vivid as possible. Challenge them to include rhyming descriptions such as 'neat on his feet' or alliteration such as 'gentle giant of the jungle'.

- Share some of the ideas the learners have come up with.

## Main activities

- Display and read an enlarged version of photocopiable page 133. Model filling it in with your ideas, linking back to the learners' suggestions from the Starter activity.

- Discuss how poems have far fewer words than a story. The words chosen have to be the best at explaining and describing.

- Remind the learners they can describe the animal using a pronoun – he / she – or give it a name to develop its character.

- Hand out individual copies of photocopiable page 133 and ask the learners to use the page to capture their ideas for words and phrases to describe an animal of their choice.

- When they're ready, encourage the learners to begin putting words and phrases together to create a poem of four to six lines.

## Plenary

- Encourage the learners to fine-tune their poems by reading what they have written so far.

- Working in groups of three or four, the learners should read each other's drafts and offer:
  - suggestion for improvements
  - help with finding a rhyming word / couplet
  - help adding a simile or metaphor where appropriate.

- When the learners are happy with their final version, allow any confident learners an opportunity to share their poem with the rest of the class.

## Success criteria

Ask the learners:

- What poetic devices have you used to describe your animal?
- What is the best line / section in your poem? Why?
- What is a pronoun? Give an example.
- How did you help another learner with their poem?

## Ideas for differentiation

**Support:** Organise these learners to work in a group supported by an adult helper and produce a shared poem.

**Extension:** Encourage these learners to consider the audience for their poem – is it going to entertain and be funny / is it for a child?

Name: _____

# Writing frame for a poem

Use this writing frame to collect vocabulary and poetic phrases that you will use to write an animal poem. Some examples have been given for you.

| Type of animal: | |
|---|---|
| **How does it move?** (For example: 'as graceful as a dancer') | |
| **How does it sound?** (For example: 'with a roar of thunder') | |
| **How do other animals feel about it?** | |
| **Is there anything special about it?** | |
| **Any other descriptions?** (For example: 'fur as soft as …') | |

# Unit assessment

### Questions to ask

- What clues in a poem tell you where it is set or where it was written?
- What do you think makes one poem better than another?
- What patterns have you seen or read in poems?

- What are poetic devices? Give some examples.
- What sort of effects do poetic devices have on the reader?
- What are the main differences between stories and poems?

## Summative assessment activities

Observe the learners while they play these games. You will quickly be able to identify those who appear to be confident and those who may need additional support.

### Simile game

This game will demonstrate how well the learners can create similes.

**You will need:**

A dice for each pair of learners; strips of paper; the following key displayed: 1 = small, 2 = strong, 3 = cold, 4 = wet, 5 = tired, 6 = dry.

**What to do**

- Ask the learners to work in pairs and give each pair a dice.

- Ask the learners to roll the dice and look at the key and then write a simile on one of the strips of paper using the word in the key, for example if they roll a 3 they might write 'as cold as ice'.

- If the learners roll the same number twice they can use a synonym for the word, for example 'sleepy' rather than 'tired'.

- Allow the pairs five minutes to write as many similes as possible, then gather all the similes for the same or similar words and display them together.

### Hidden in a poem!

During this activity the learners will be able to demonstrate their understanding of the technical features and vocabulary associated with poetry.

**You will need:**

Five different poems from different cultures – enough copies for the learners to share them between themselves amicably.

**What to do**

- Ask the learners to look through the poems for examples of the following poetic elements:
  - theme
  - setting
  - patterns
  - poetic devices.

- Ask the learners to write a note against each heading for each poem, providing detail about what is used in the poem, for example: 'Theme – friendship', 'Patterns – rhyming couplets'.

- When the learners have completed the task for each poem, ask them to spend time sharing their findings and examples.

### Written assessment

Provide the learners with photocopiable pages 124 and 135 and ask them to answer the questions about 'My Sari' by Debjani Chatterjee.

Name: _____

# 'My Sari' by Debjani Chatterjee

Read the poem again and answer these questions:

1. What is the rhyming pattern in this poem?

   _____

   _____

2. Who do you think is the voice of the poem? Try to describe them.

   _____

   _____

3. What do you think, 'It wraps around me like sunshine' might mean?

   _____

   _____

4. There are many vibrant descriptions in the poem. Draw what you can 'see' in the poem and add the words and phrases from the poem as labels to the drawing.

## Reading and reviewing

### Learning objectives

● Read and comment on different books by the same author. (3Rf10)
● Write book reviews summarising what a book is about. (3Wn1)
● Use knowledge of punctuation and grammar to read age-appropriate texts with fluency, understanding and expression. (3GPr1)

### Resources

Photocopiable page 137; *The Tunnel, Willy the Wimp, Into the Forest* and *Gorilla* by Anthony Browne (Walker Books) or another collection of picture books with an adventure theme; internet access.

### Starter

• Display a collection of Anthony Browne picture books. Ask: *Does anyone know this author?*
• Look at the front covers of the books together and share what the learners know about Anthony Browne's books. Search for information about him online (for example at www.childrenslaureate.org.uk/previous-laureates/anthony-browne).
• Give the learners an opportunity to browse through the books and select a book to read with a partner.
• Remind the learners to look out for clues as to how to use their voice when reading, for example commas, question marks and full stops.
• Tell the learners to collect information about Anthony Browne from the internet to form a class display.

### Main activities

• Give the learners time to read and enjoy the illustrations in their chosen book by Anthony Browne.
• Display an enlarged version of photocopiable page 137.
• Discuss what a book review is. Explain that the learners are free to express their likes and dislikes about books they have read. Explain that we often choose a particular book because somebody has recommended it to us.

• Tell the learners you will leave copies of the review page in the book / library corner for the learners to fill in when they want to recommend a book to another learner.
• Briefly collect the learners' ideas about the books in this selection that they have read.
• Ask: *Which books include an adventure?* (All.) *What are the themes?* (Family, seeing something from someone else's point of view, misunderstandings in families.) *Do the stories have a happy ending?* (Yes, they all do.)
• Distribute individual copies of photocopiable page 137 and ask the learners to work in pairs to fill in the book review for the book they have just read together.

### Plenary

• Organise the learners into teams who have read the same book by Anthony Browne.
• Encourage them to work together to explain why their book is great and should be read by the rest of the class. Ask them to consider the illustrations and what they add to the story, how exciting the adventure is, and what they think of the ending.
• Tell each team to nominate a speaker. Explain there are no winners as they are all great books!

### Success criteria

Ask the learners:

● What sort of information should be included in a book review?
● What similarities did you notice between the Anthony Browne books?
● Explain the theme in the book you read.

### Ideas for differentiation

**Support:** If possible, read one or two of the books for this lesson in advance with these learners to support them.

**Extension:** Encourage these learners to routinely write reviews for books they have read, extending to reviewing longer chapter books.

Name: _____

# Book review

Use this table to write a review of a book you have read.

| Name of book: | Author: |
|---|---|
| What kind of story is it (myth, adventure, animal, fantasy, and so on)? | |
| Why did you choose it (recommended by a friend, liked the cover, and so on)? | |
| What do you like or dislike about the story? | |
| What is the best part of the story? Why? | |
| How does the story make you feel? | |
| Why would you recommend it to a friend? | |
| Does this book make you want to read other books by the same author? Why? | |
| How many stars would you give it? Colour in the number of stars. | ☆ ☆ ☆ ☆ ☆ |

# Features of an adventure story

- Identify different types of stories and typical story themes. (3Rf5)
- Make a record of information drawn from a text, e.g. by completing a chart. (3Wn4)

Photocopiable page 139; *Into the Forest* by Anthony Browne (Walker Books) or another adventure story.

## Starter

- Tell the learners to discuss the word 'adventure'. Ask: *What does it mean? What should we expect from an adventure story?* (Excitement, tension, danger, a dilemma, a brave character, something a bit frightening, a happy ending, and so on.)
- Look at the cover of *Into the Forest* by Anthony Browne or your own adventure story. Ask: *What sort of adventure do you think this will be about?*
- Read the book and pause occasionally to make sure the learners have an opportunity to see the details in the illustrations.

## Main activities

- Tell the learners they are fast becoming experts on Anthony Browne's books and adventure stories!
- Create with the learners a list of key features of adventure stories based on their reading so far:
  - The main characters are often children.
  - There is an element of excitement.
  - There is often a bad character providing the problem.
  - It is important that the reader finds out about how the characters are feeling.
  - The setting is very important in building up the excitement.
  - The story usually starts in a happy, safe place, moves to the adventure and then returns to the happy, safe place.
- Display the key features for the learners to refer back to.

- Distribute individual copies of photocopiable page 139 and discuss the features listed and any unfamiliar vocabulary with the learners.
- Ask the learners to use details from two adventure stories they've read recently (and have access to), including *Into the Forest* if possible, to fill in the table.

## Plenary

- Invite the learners working on the Extension activity to tell the rest of the learners a bit more about the problem section. Ask: *What is the problem in* Into the Forest? *He is missing his dad? He gets lost in the forest? The grandma is sick?*
- Introduce the dilemma: *Should he have tried to help the lost children in the forest?* Divide the learners into pairs to discuss the moral dilemma he faces.

Ask the learners:

- What features tell us a story is an adventure story?
- In *Into the Forest*, how does the setting change as the story goes on?
- How do the illustrations help build up the tension?
- Explain the boy's dilemma about which way to go – the long or short way?

**Support:** Ask these learners to work in a small adult-helper led group with an enlarged version of photocopiable page 139. Ask the group to collect the features collaboratively using words, phrases and pictures.

**Extension:** Ask these learners to explain the problem part of *Into the Forest* in more detail by eliciting some of the inferred meanings.

Name: _____

# Finding the key features of an adventure story

Use this table to capture the main features of two adventure stories you've read.

| Name of book | | | |
|---|---|---|---|
| Information about the main characters: How do they look, behave and feel during the story? | | | |
| Information about the setting at the beginning, middle and end of the story. | | | |
| Information about the problem. | | | |
| Most exciting part of the book: Where is the tension at its highest? | | | |

# Mapping an adventure story

- Identify the main points or gist of a text. (3Rf6)
- Make a record of information drawn from a text, e.g. by completing a chart. (3Wn4)

Photocopiable page 141; copies of *Into the Forest* by Anthony Browne (Walker Books) or another adventure story with a simple structure.

## Starter

- Explain to the learners that they are going to write adventure stories eventually, and to be able to write a good adventure story they need to think about how these stories are put together.
- Display the headings 'Introduction', 'Problem', 'Adventure' and 'Ending' on the board.
- Give the learners a few minutes to discuss these headings with a partner. What do they think happens in each section? Ask: *Which section will be the longest?*

## Main activities

- Discuss each of the headings in more detail and let the learners contribute their ideas. Capture their ideas on the board until you have something like this:
  - Introduction: this is the section where the reader learns about the characters and where the story is set.
  - Problem: a problem is introduced and the effects of the problem mean something needs to happen.
  - Adventure: this is where the characters have an adventure (often involving a journey of some kind). During the adventure the problem is sorted out.
  - Ending: the story usually returns to the setting from the beginning. The ending is usually happy!

- Ask the learners to work in pairs. Distribute to each pair photocopiable page 141 and copies of *Into the Forest* by Anthony Browne, or another adventure story you've been reading together. Ask the pairs to make notes on the photocopiable page about what happens in each section of the story. Tell them that they will need to make decisions about when one section ends and another begins.

## Plenary

- Collect the learners' ideas about how they organised their structure and how they decided which bit went where.
- Allow them to discuss differing answers and explain there is no exact right or wrong answer. Explain that there will be differences of opinion, but ask the learners to justify their reasons.

Ask the learners:

- Explain the structure of an adventure story.
- What do we learn about the boy in the introduction?
- What is the problem in this story?
- What happens to the boy on his journey?
- Describe the difference between the setting at the start of the story and the setting at the end of the story.

**Support:** Give these learners a copy of the book with sticky notes separating the four sections to help them choose what to write in each section.

**Extension:** Tell these learners to include details of the dilemma the boy faces in the wood in the adventure part of the story.

Name: _____

# Mapping an adventure story

Think about the adventure story you have read and make notes about what happens in each part of the story.

**Introduction** (the reader first learns about the characters and setting)

_____

_____

_____

_____

**Problem** (a problem is introduced and the reader learns how it affects the characters)

_____

_____

_____

_____

**Adventure** (the character has an adventure, often involving a journey of some kind; during the adventure the problem is sorted out)

_____

_____

_____

**Ending** (a happy outcome back at the original setting)

_____

_____

_____

_____

# Creating a mood graph

## Learning objectives

● Infer the meaning of unknown words from the context. (3PSV12)

● Consider words that make an impact, e.g. adjectives and powerful verbs. (3Rf7)

● Begin to infer meanings beyond the literal, e.g. about motives and character. (3Rf4)

## Resources

Photocopiable page 143; copies of *Into the Forest* by Anthony Browne (Walker Books) or another adventure story with a simple structure.

## Starter

• Read *Into the Forest* by Anthony Browne; the learners should now be fairly familiar with the text and its structure.

• Elicit the mood of the book. Ask: *How do you feel about the characters and setting?*

• Show the learners the page with the 'I miss Dad' notes. Ask: *What is the mood here?*

• Elicit synonyms for their suggestions to extend their vocabulary choices, for example: 'ecstatic', 'thrilled', 'on top of the world', 'elated' or 'unhappy', 'sorrowful', 'miserable', 'down', 'sorry', 'heartbroken'.

• Discuss how these words give more details about the feelings.

## Main activities

• Ask: *Does each page say how the boy is feeling?* (No.) *How can we tell how he is feeling?* Discuss the term 'infer' and explain how we learn about a character's feelings from how they behave or move or from their actions.

• Display an enlarged version of photocopiable page 143.

• Tell the learners to watch as you trace your finger from the bottom to the top of the vertical axis. Explain that the bottom of the graph represents the saddest part of the story and the top represents the happiest.

• Skim through the book and briefly match up the notes along the bottom of the graph with the pages in the book.

• Model plotting the level of feelings on the graph, for example in the first column the noise in the night would make the mood sad, so draw a horizontal line above 'thunder and lightning' at the lowest point.

• Draw a slightly higher line for 'Quick way to Grandma's' to represent the boy looking forward to seeing his grandma.

• Distribute individual copies of photocopiable page 143 and ask the learners to plot the mood for each event, starting with their own thoughts about the first two events.

## Plenary

• Tell the learners to work with a partner and compare their levels on the graphs, then join another pair and compare again.

• Discuss any major differences in their levels and explain there will always be some variation when interpreting feelings.

## Success criteria

Ask the learners:

● Is the story happy or sad?

● How do we learn about the mood of a story?

● How does the mood change during a story?

● Give me some words to describe a happy mood.

## Ideas for differentiation

**Support:** Give these learners a copy of the book to support organising their ideas.

**Extension:** Tell these learners to add mood words for each event along the graph.

Name: _____

# Creating a mood graph

Plot the key events in **Into the Forest** by Anthony Browne against the appropriate mood to create a graph for the story.

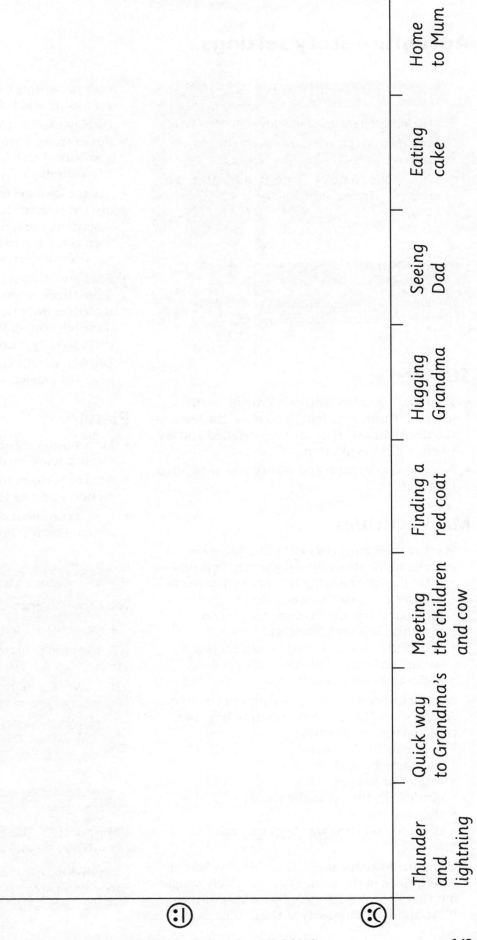

| Thunder and lightning | Quick way to Grandma's | Meeting the children and cow | Finding a red coat | Hugging Grandma | Seeing Dad | Eating cake | Home to Mum |
|---|---|---|---|---|---|---|---|

☺

😐

☹

# Adventure story settings

## Learning objectives

- Develop descriptions of settings in stories. (3Wf2)
- Consider how choice of words can heighten meaning. (3PSV11)
- Choose and compare words to strengthen the impact of writing, including noun phrases. (3Wf10)

## Resources

*The Tunnel* by Anthony Browne (Walker Books); sticky notes; photocopiable page 145.

## Starter

- Read *The Tunnel* by Anthony Browne to the learners. Pause occasionally to show the learners the illustrations – they are very detailed and are worth a close inspection.
- Pause also to explain and clarify any unfamiliar language.

## Main activities

- Support the learners by briefly clarifying the events and the structure. Ask them to explain the:
  - introduction (meeting the main characters – brother and sister, Jack and Rose)
  - problem (they don't get on; they go out together; Jack goes missing)
  - adventure (Rose is scared but enters the tunnel and finds and saves Jack)
  - ending (they become friends).
- Ask the learners about the settings in the story. Ask them to discuss possible vocabulary that could be used to describe:
  - Rose and Jack's home
  - the waste ground
  - inside the tunnel
  - outside the tunnel in the wood
  - the clearing
  - the wood on their way back through
  - home.
- Using the learners' suggestions, discuss how the descriptions of the settings are relatively simple, but that we can infer more by looking at the illustrations (look closely at the double page

with no writing), including how the characters are feeling and behaving.

- Display two contrasting settings from the book (for example Rose running through the wood and both the children back at home after the adventure).
- Ask the learners to work with a partner to discuss each of the two settings and write words describing them on sticky notes. They should then come out to the front and put them under the relevant setting.
- Read and discuss their ideas, modelling turning some single words into short descriptive sentences (for example 'scary, dark, creepy' into 'Rose felt scared, the wood was dark, she felt like there were eyes everywhere').
- Distribute individual copies of photocopiable page 145 and ask the learners complete the task.

## Plenary

- Model using the some of the learners' ideas to create a sentence describing one of the settings.
- Ask the learners to work with a partner to create an oral sentence to describe either setting.
- Give a confident pair of learners an opportunity to share their sentence with the rest of the class.

## Success criteria

Ask the learners:

- What is a setting?
- How can you use your senses to describe a setting?
- Why is it important to give interesting descriptions of settings?
- How can the description of a setting change how we feel about the character?

## Ideas for differentiation

**Support:** Ask these learners to write single words and phrases to describe the settings.

**Extension:** Ask these learners to use their ideas to write a paragraph for each setting.

Name: _____

# Two very different settings

Try to imagine what Rose could see, hear, feel, smell and perhaps taste in these settings.

1.  **Home** (when Rose is at home reading)

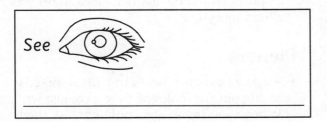

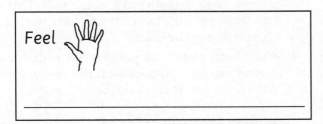

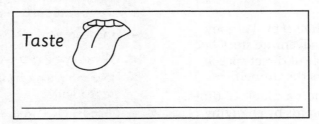

2.  **The tunnel** (when Rose is crawling through the tunnel)

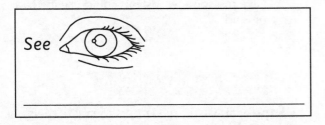

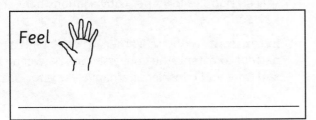

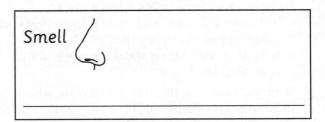

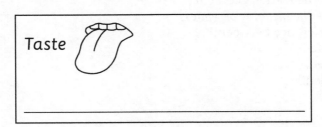

# Dialogue and direct speech

● Use reading as a model for writing dialogue. (3Wf8)

● Explore vocabulary for introducing and concluding dialogue, e.g. said, asked. (3PSV13)

● Adapt tone of voice, use of vocabulary and non-verbal features for different audiences. (3SL2)

**Resources**

*The Tunnel* by Anthony Brown (Walker Books) or another adventure story; photocopiable page 147.

## Starter

• Display a page from *The Tunnel* by Anthony Browne, or from another adventure story book, which includes an example of direct speech (possibly where Jack enters the tunnel).

• Read the page to the learners a couple of times, emphasising the spoken words by changing your voice for each character. Read the text again and ask the learners to join in.

• Ask: *How do we know when to put on a voice for Jack or Rose?* (Direct speech marks.)

• Ask: *What does the writer do so that we don't get confused as to who is speaking?*

## Main activities

• Discuss the 'rules' for direct speech or dialogue:
  • Spoken words go inside speech marks
  • Start a new line for each new person speaking
  • Put punctuation inside the speech marks
  • Tell the reader who is speaking (for example 'answered the boy').

• Briefly discuss the rule about knowing who is speaking and overuse of the word 'said'. What other words for 'said' can the learners come up with? Ask: *Will this change the meaning of what is being said?* Discuss the difference between:
  • "Come here!" she shouted.
  • "Come here," she giggled.
  • "Come here," she pleaded.

• Distribute individual copies of photocopiable page 147 and explain that it provides two conversations from the book set out in speech bubbles, which the learners need to reset as direct speech.

## Plenary

• Ask the learners to work in pairs to practise acting out the dialogue they have just written. When they are feeling confident, ask them to perform their dialogue to another pair. This will help them see how the characters are feeling when they say the lines.

• When both pairs have performed the dialogue, ask the two pairs to decide on the best word to replace 'said' in their dialogue.

**Success criteria**

Ask the learners:

● Why do writers use direct speech in stories?

● How can we recognise direct speech when we are reading?

● What can we do to make the direct speech stand out when we are reading to others?

● What are the rules for direct speech?

● Give me some verbs you could use instead of 'said'.

**Ideas for differentiation**

**Support:** Ask these learners to create their own speech bubbles for other conversations between Jack and Rose.

**Extension:** Ask these learners to work with a partner to extend the conversations between Jack and Rose and consider alternative verbs for 'said'.

# Speech bubbles and direct speech

Rewrite these conversations using the 'rules' for direct speech.

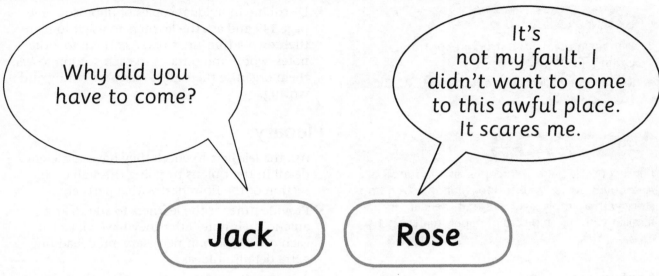

Why did you have to come?

**Jack**

It's not my fault. I didn't want to come to this awful place. It scares me.

**Rose**

_____

_____

_____

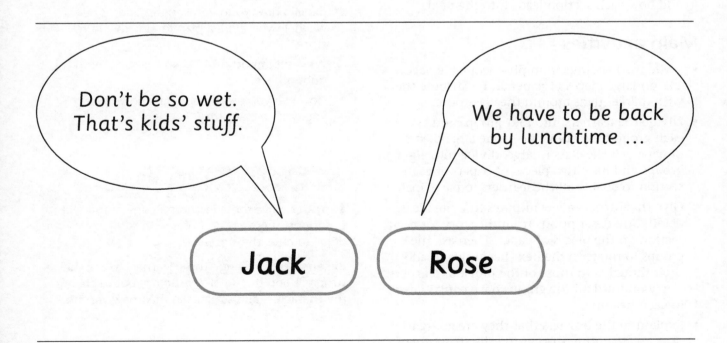

Don't be so wet. That's kids' stuff.

**Jack**

We have to be back by lunchtime ...

**Rose**

_____

_____

_____

# Planning an adventure story

- Plan main points as a structure for story writing. (3Wf5)
- Identify the main points or gist of a text. (3Rf6)

Photocopiable page 149; copies of *The Tunnel* by Anthony Browne (Walker Books) or an adventure story with a simple structure that the learners are familiar with; large pieces of paper; marker pens.

## Starter

- Show the learners the cover of *The Tunnel* by Anthony Browne, or one of your adventure stories, and explain that they are going to plan an adventure story using this book as a model.
- Display an enlarged version of photocopiable page 149 and explain how the flowchart works and how each section leads into the next.

## Main activities

- Write the headings from photocopiable page 149 on large pieces of paper and distribute them with marker pens around the classroom.
- Divide the learners into four groups and ask each group to start by one of the large pieces of paper. (If the class is large, divide into eight groups and have two pieces of paper for each section to enable all the learners to participate.)
- Give the learners a few minutes to write ideas, details and descriptions from the story for their section on the pieces of paper. Then ask the groups to rotate to the next heading and add their thoughts to those of the previous learners. Carry on until all the groups have contributed to each heading.
- Explain to the learners that they are going to plan an adventure story using the structure of *The Tunnel* (or your chosen adventure story) to help them. (Some of the learners can simply retell it, others can make changes to the names of the characters, the settings, and so on, depending on ability.)

- Distribute individual copies of photocopiable page 149 and ask the learners to use it to plan their own adventure story. Ask them to write notes, words and phrases in each section to help them organise their ideas ready for telling and writing.

## Plenary

- Ask the learners to check they have sufficient detail in their plans by going through each section of the flowchart with a partner.
- Provide time for the learners to add to and amend their notes after they have looked at each other's plan. If necessary, model adding extra details or ideas.
- Ask a confident learner to explain their story using their plan.

Ask the learners:

- How and why do we plan stories?
- Explain how your words, notes and phrases will help you write a plan for an adventure story.
- Why is it important to keep the sections in the right order?
- How can you use a story you know to help you write a new story?

**Support:** Give these learners a copy of the text to support them taking notes with sufficient detail to retell the story.

**Extension:** Challenge these learners to use the structure and theme of *The Tunnel*, but to change the characters and settings in their new version.

Name: _____

# Planning frame for an adventure story

Use this flowchart to organise your ideas for a new adventure story.

**Introduction** (introduce the characters and setting)

**Problem** (introduce the problem and explain how the problem affects the characters)

**Adventure** (take the characters on an adventure to sort out the problem)

**Ending** (explain how the story ends with the characters back in a safe setting)

# Telling an adventure story

- Identify pronouns and understand their function in a sentence. (3GPr4)
- Begin to adapt movement to create a character in drama. (3SL7)
- Practise to improve performance when reading aloud. (3SL6)

Photocopiable pages 149 (completed) and 151.

## Starter

- Discuss the term 'pronoun', including how and where pronouns are used.
- Agree that pronouns replace nouns, and ask the learners to give you examples of pronouns ('I', 'you', 'he', 'she', 'it', 'we', 'they', 'me', 'him', 'her', 'us', 'them').
- Distribute photocopiable page 151 to the learners in pairs. Discuss it and elicit from the learners that there are too many Jacks and Roses in each paragraph.
- Ask the learners to work with their partner to cross out some of the nouns and replace them with appropriate pronouns to improve each paragraph.

## Main activities

- Explain to the learners that they will use their plans from the previous lesson to tell their stories.
- Ask them to work in pairs, taking it in turns to tell their partner their adventure story. Remind them to use their plan on photocopiable page 149 and to consider:
  - how they can use their voice to interest and excite the listeners
  - pausing between each section to show the different stages in the story
  - using appropriate actions to keep the listeners engaged.

- Demonstrate a few actions from *The Tunnel* to give the learners some ideas for their storytelling, for example opening and closing a book to symbolise starting and ending a story, hugging yourself when Rose is scared and does not know whether to go into the tunnel or not, tapping all over your body to show the statue turning back into Jack.

## Plenary

- Give the learners an opportunity to share their story by telling it to another learner. Tell the listeners to look out for a good mixture of nouns and pronouns being used and to check that the story flows according to the adventure-story structure.
- Ask a couple of the more confident learners to tell all or part of their story to the rest of the class and model giving positive feedback.

Ask the learners:

- Why do we use a mixture of pronouns and nouns in our stories?
- What strategies can you use when telling an oral story to keep the listener engaged and interested?
- How did you use your voice and actions when telling your adventure story?

**Support:** Provide these learners with key sentence openers to help them focus on what they will say in each section, for example: 'Once upon a time …', 'The brother and sister didn't get on at all …', 'Rose felt very scared about going into the tunnel', and so on.

**Extension:** Challenge these learners to make the dilemma part of the story very clear, with their main characters struggling to know what to do.

Name: _____

# Pronouns

Pronouns are words that replace a noun (naming word).
Use these pronouns to replace the nouns in the paragraphs below.

| I | you | he | she | it | we |
|---|---|---|---|---|---|
| they | me | him | her | us | them |

At night Jack slept soundly in his room, but Rose would lie awake,

listening to the noises of the night. Sometimes Jack crept into

Rose's room to frighten Rose, for Jack knew that Rose was afraid

of the dark.

Rose was frightened of the tunnel and so Rose waited for Jack to

come out again. Rose waited and waited, but Jack did not come.

Rose was close to tears. What could Rose do? Rose had to follow

Jack into the tunnel.

Adapted from **The Tunnel** by Anthony Browne

# Writing an adventure story

- Begin to organise writing in sections or paragraphs in extended stories. (3Wf6)
- Use reading as a model for writing dialogue. (3Wf8)
- Establish purpose for writing, using features and style based on model texts. (3Wn2)

**Resources**

Photocopiable pages 149 and 153; scissors.

## Starter

- Cut out and display enlarged versions of the pictures from photocopiable page 153.
- Ask the learners to work in pairs to write a short conversation between the two brothers for one of the pictures, role-playing the conversation before writing it down.
- Explain that the dialogue should give information about how the characters are feeling in that part of the story.
- Remind the learners that they should be using the correct punctuation in their dialogues. (See the rules for direct speech on page 146.)
- Give a few pairs of learners an opportunity to share their dialogue with the rest of the class.

## Main activities

- Tell the learners that they are going to use the pictures to write their own adventure story. Ask: *What will happen inside the spooky house? What will happen to one of the brothers? Who will they meet or what will they find? How will it all be resolved?* Give the learners a few minutes to discuss ideas with their partner.
- Hand out individual copies of photocopiable pages 149 and 153 and ask the learners to plan their own story. How exciting can they make it?

- Discuss how Anthony Browne uses illustrations to support his stories by taking the reader to different places. Ask: *How could we use the illustrations to help us?* Discuss the different options:
  - no illustrations – the reader must use their imagination
  - just one picture – perhaps at the end of the story to tie up the ending
  - completely illustrated – perhaps with some elements of the story only existing in the illustrations
  - illustrations part coloured for emphasis (as in *Into the Forest*).
- Ask the learners to write a first draft of their story, sticking in the pictures from the photocopiable page or adding their own where appropriate. Remind them to use direct speech.

## Plenary

- Tell the learners to display their first drafts on their desks and give the class an opportunity to see how each has used the illustrations.
- Discuss what has been seen and how the learners have used any illustrations.

**Success criteria**

Ask the learners:

- What is direct speech? Why do writers use it?
- What are the rules?
- What are illustrations?
- How does Anthony Browne use illustrations in his books?
- How do illustrations affect the story?

**Ideas for differentiation**

**Support:** Ask these learners to write a sentence about each picture to create a short story.

**Extension:** Ask these learners to use the adventure-story structure to create a book with chapters and illustrations.

# Two brothers

Cut out these pictures and use them to help you write an adventure story about two brothers.

# Editing and improving an adventure story

## Learning objectives

- Use ICT to write, edit and present work. (3Wp4)
- Establish purpose for writing, using features and style based on model texts. (3Wn2)

## Resources

Photocopiable pages 153 and 155; completed first draft of the story from the previous lesson; access to computers for all the learners; glue.

## Starter

- Discuss the first draft of the adventure story that the learners wrote in the previous lesson. Ask: *What should the success criteria be for your adventure story?*
- Distribute photocopiable page 155. Go through each point and make sure the learners know what they need to do to write a successful adventure story.

## Main activities

- Explain to the learners that they are going to write their final version of their story using ICT. Ask: *How should we organise the sections?*
- Tell the learners that the four sections make the story at least four chapters long, however the adventure part of the story may be longer and need two chapters.
- Discuss options for an attractively presented story such as: leaving a double line space between the sections, giving the chapters titles, inserting an illustration at the end of each section.
- Let the learners sketch out how the book will be laid out. Remind them that they will need to leave space to glue the illustrations in later.
- Model using the word-processing software to check spelling, using the dictionary and thesaurus, using a larger font for the chapter heads, leaving space for illustrations, and so on.

- Allow time and support for the learners to write a final version of their story on the computer.
- When they've finished, tell the learners to check their story against the success criteria on photocopiable page 155. Allow them to make final changes before printing off the final version and sticking in the pictures.

## Plenary

- Ask the learners to share their story with a partner and ask the partners to check the stories against the success criteria.
- Celebrate the successes in writing the adventure stories by creating a library-style display of 'Adventure stories' using the finished books and the Anthony Browne books. Encourage the learners to read each other's stories.

## Success criteria

Ask the learners:

- How have you organised each section in your adventure story?
- What changes have you made to improve your story?
- What have you identified as good in someone else's story?
- What strategies have you used to keep the reader's interest?
- How have you used pictures and drawings to enhance your story?

## Ideas for differentiation

**Support:** Organise these learners to work in a small adult-helper led group to produce a collaborative story using the pictures from photocopiable page 153.

**Extension:** Encourage these learners to turn their story into a book by drawing a front cover and writing a blurb.

Name: _____

# Adventure story success criteria

Use this table to check your adventure story. Ask your partner to check it too.

| Success criteria | Author | Partner |
|---|---|---|
| I have included a title for the story. | | |
| I have included a good clear introduction to the characters and setting. | | |
| I have explained the problem. | | |
| The characters have gone on an adventure to solve the problem. | | |
| I have explained how the story ends (happily). | | |
| I have used some direct speech. | | |
| I have used a mixture of nouns and pronouns in my sentences. | | |
| I have explained how my characters are feeling by what they say and do. | | |
| Read your story and explain two things you did really well and one thing that could be improved. | ☆ _____ <br><br> _____ <br><br> ☆ _____ <br><br> _____ <br><br> Next time ... <br><br> _____ <br><br> _____ | ☆ _____ <br><br> _____ <br><br> ☆ _____ <br><br> _____ <br><br> Next time ... <br><br> _____ <br><br> _____ |

# Unit assessment

## Questions to ask

- What is a book review and what sort of information should you find in one?
- Explain some of the similarities and some of the differences between the Anthony Browne books you have read during this unit.
- What have you enjoyed about reading and writing adventure stories?

- Explain the structure writers use for adventure stories.
- What strategies can you use when telling an oral story to keep the listener engaged and interested?

## Summative assessment activities

Observe the learners while they play these games. You will quickly be able to identify those who appear to be confident and those who may need additional support.

### Settings game

This activity encourages the learners to use their imagination to create interesting and exciting settings.

**You will need:**

Photocopiable page 157; scissors; large pieces of paper; marker pens.

**What to do**

- Cut out the settings cards from photocopiable page 157.
- Organise the learners into small groups and give each group a set of cards.
- Ask each group to pick one card at a time and see how many ideas they can come up with for a story or description of a setting. Ask them to write these on the large pieces of paper using the marker pens.

### Quick plays

This activity encourages the learners to use the adventure story structure to create a short play.

**You will need:**

Photocopiable page 157; scissors; two hats; some space for the learners to act out short plays.

**What to do**

- Briefly review and discuss the adventure-story structure the learners have been using.
- Organise the learners into small groups.
- Place the setting and problem ideas from photocopiable page 157 into two separate hats. Ask someone from each group to pick a card from each hat.
- Tell the groups to use their setting and problem to create a short play using the adventure-story structure they have been studying.
- Let the learners take it in turns to act out their adventure stories to another group or to the rest of the class, depending on how confident they feel.

## Written assessment

Tell the learners to choose one of the adventure books they have enjoyed reading and to write a blurb for it. Remind them not to retell the story, but to give enough information to draw the reader in, including using questions.

# Adventure cards

## Settings

| | | |
|---|---|---|
| A forest | A shed | A walled garden |
| A hidden cupboard | A secret passage | A swamp |
| The basket of a hot-air balloon | An empty house | A book shop |

## Problem ideas

| | |
|---|---|
| finding someone | hiding something |
| finding something | searching for something |
| losing something | searching for someone |

# Unit 3B: Non-chronological reports

## Finding books in libraries

### Learning objectives

- Understand and use the terms 'fact', 'fiction' and 'non-fiction'. (3Rf8)
- Locate books by classification. (3Rn5)

### Resources

Photocopiable page 159; access to the school or public / community library.

## Starter

- Ask the learners: *What is a library? What should we expect to find there?*
- Discuss how libraries are not necessarily just about borrowing books. People can borrow other items too such as DVDs and CDs, and many libraries also provide computer access.
- Ask: *Are there any rules for being in a library?* Briefly discuss the etiquette of speaking in hushed tones so as not to disturb others, putting books back where they came from, speaking politely to library staff, and so on.
- Take the learners to either a school or public / community library. Elicit from the learners how the books are organised into different sections.

## Main activities

- When you first arrive at the library, give the learners an opportunity to have a quick look around and get a feel for the place and how the books have been arranged, displayed and organised.
- Ask: *What have you found or noticed about the books?*
- Establish that the books are organised into fiction and non-fiction. The fiction is organised by authors' names; the non-fiction is usually organised by subject.
- Model how to use this organisation to quickly find what you are looking for.
- Explain that without a system you could be wandering around a library all day and still not find what you are looking for!

- Distribute photocopiable page 159 to the learners in pairs.
- Tell the learners to work with their partner to find books that fit the descriptions on the photocopiable page. Remind them to note down the title and author of each book they find. (Organise the learners to start at different points in the list.)

## Plenary

- Display an enlarged version of photocopiable page 159 and collect the names of books the learners found, giving each pair an opportunity to respond.
- Discuss any duplicated answers. This will largely depend on the size and range of books available in the library, however the activity should highlight that there is a huge range of books available in a library compared to a home or the classroom.
- Collect the learners' responses to the two questions at the bottom of the photocopiable page.

### Success criteria

Ask the learners:

- What is a library?
- Who is allowed to use it?
- How are the books organised and displayed?
- How can you quickly find exactly what you want in a library?

### Ideas for differentiation

**Support:** Ask these learners to work in a small adult-helper led group to complete the photocopiable page.

**Extension:** Give these learners an additional challenge of finding books that fit new categories, for example books about sea life, or another specific topic.

Name: _____

# Organising books in a library

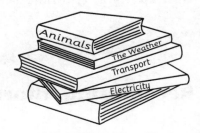

1.  Use your knowledge of how library books are organised to find the following books.

|  | Name of book and author | Fiction (F) or Non-fiction (N) |
|---|---|---|
| A book by Anthony Browne |  |  |
| A book by Roald Dahl |  |  |
| A book about pets |  |  |
| A book of poems |  |  |
| A history book |  |  |
| A hobbies book |  |  |
| A book for a young reader |  |  |
| A Science book |  |  |
| A book about different religions |  |  |

2.  Which book was the easiest to find?

_____

3.  Why do you think that was?

_____

# Recognising information texts

## Learning objectives

● Locate information in non-fiction texts using contents page and index. (3Rn2)

● Locate books by classification. (3Rn5)

● Consider ways that information is set out on page and on screen, e.g. lists, charts, bullet points. (3Rn4)

## Resources

Photocopiable page 161; scissors; a variety of non-fiction texts (enough for one for each learner) linked to another curriculum area such as History; a hat.

## Starter

• Discuss the different types of non-fiction texts that the learners found at the library: biographies, instruction manuals and information books.

• Explain that for the rest of the unit they will learn about the features of information books, which are sometimes called 'report texts'. These are texts that give straight information, and often it doesn't matter if you don't read all the information. If it's a book, it often isn't read from front to back in the way that fiction, biographies or instructions are, but instead the reader searches for the section that they are interested in.

• Create cards from an enlarged copy of photocopiable page 161.

• Ask the learners to give you examples of the features of information or report texts. As they identify key features, reveal and display the relevant card.

• Repeat until the learners run out of ideas, then show and explain any remaining cards.

• Discuss that not all report texts will have all of these features.

## Main activities

• Distribute a variety of suitable report texts (books, or print-outs from the internet also work well for this activity).

• Distribute photocopiable page 161 to the learners in pairs and tell them to work together to find each feature on the page in one of the report texts on their desks. Explain that they are not expected to read the reports.

• If the learners disagree about any of the features, ask them to discuss it in the Plenary.

## Plenary

• Briefly discuss any misconceptions that have arisen during the Main activity.

• Either as a whole class or in small groups, play a game of 'Guess who.' Put the cards from photocopiable page 161 that were used in the Starter activity into a hat. Ask the learners to take turns to pick a card out of the hat and describe it without saying the word / phrase. Can the other learners guess what it is?

## Success criteria

Ask the learners:

● Tell me five features you would expect to find in a report text.

● What's the difference between a diagram, a map and an illustration?

● How can a glossary help the reader?

● What effect do different size and style fonts have on the reader?

## Ideas for differentiation

**Support:** Organise these learners to work in a small adult-helper led group to identify the features of a report text. Use the cards as page markers for future reference.

**Extension:** Ask these learners to create a poster with definitions and examples of the key features of report texts to use as reference and display.

# Key features of report texts

Can you find these features in one of the report texts you've been given?
Cut out the cards and make a pile of the features you find and a pile
of the features you don't find.

| | | |
|---|---|---|
| contents | index | glossary |
| photographs | illustrations | diagrams |
| maps | charts | headings |
| sub headings | captions | labels |
| bullet points | different style fonts | different size fonts |

# Skimming and scanning

## Learning objectives

- Consider ways that information is set out on page and on screen, e.g. lists, charts, bullet points. (3Rn4)
- Identify the main points or gist of a text. (3Rf6)

## Resources

Photocopiable pages 161 and 163; scissors; highlighter pens.

## Starter

- This unit can easily be adapted to suit any History or Geography topic.
- Divide the learners into groups and give each group a set of cards from photocopiable page 161. Tell them to distribute the cards evenly within their group. Ask them to read their cards and check that they know what they mean.
- Display an enlarged version of photocopiable page 163 and read it with the learners. Tell them to listen / look out for the features on their card. Tell them to hold up their card when they hear or see the relevant features, explaining and justifying their idea from the text.
- Tell them to support the rest of their group by helping other learners look out for their features.
- Discuss any of the cards that were not used. Ask: *Does it matter that these features weren't used?*

## Main activities

- Distribute individual copies of photocopiable page 163. Ask: *Is this text easy to read and follow? Why?*
- Discuss how it is possible to get the 'gist' of the text very easily. Ask: *Why is that?* (The layout with its sub-headings, pictures, use of bullet points, ideas clearly expressed, and so on.)
- Explain how we can get the gist of a text by skimming and scanning and picking out the main points. Underline the words 'Nile', 'drinking', 'cooking', 'crops', 'wash', 'livestock' and 'fish' to show how we can pick out key words.

- Ask the learners to work with their partner to rewrite photocopiable page 163 using only 25 words for the first section and 15 for the second.
- When they've finished, check that they have not changed the meaning of the text within their new version.
- Ask the learners to share their version with another pair, then try to reduce their versions to 15 words for the first section and 10 for the second.

## Plenary

- Together with the learners, create a class version of the reduced-text exercise, using the best ideas from the learners' feedback.
- Finally, tell the learners to compare this version to theirs, and ask them to consider how they did.

## Success criteria

Ask the learners:

- What does the gist of a text mean?
- How can you find the gist of a text using skimming and scanning?
- How did you select the best words when you reduced the text?
- Where else might you use this skill? (Note-taking?)

## Ideas for differentiation

**Support:** Ask these learners to use highlighter pens to pick out the key vocabulary.

**Extension:** Give these learners an opportunity to use their chosen vocabulary to explain orally the gist of the text.

# The ordinary Ancient Egyptians

## The Nile

The River Nile and the land on either side of its banks played a very important part of daily life for the ordinary Ancient Egyptians. It provided:

- water for drinking and cooking
- water to grow crops
- water to wash in
- water for livestock to drink
- fish to eat
- a way to travel, using a boat.

Once a year there would be a great flood and the banks of the Nile would burst. This made the soil rich with nutrients and ideal for growing food. Without the Nile, life for the Ancient Egyptians would have been almost impossible.

## Jobs

Most of the ordinary Ancient Egyptians would have worked in the fields on either side of the Nile, growing crops or looking after animals such as sheep and cows. The farmers grew food to eat and sell, like figs and dates, along with farming crops like wheat and barley for baking bread and beer.

# Comparing report texts

● Use ICT sources to locate simple information. (3Rn7)

● Read a range of story, poetry and information books and begin to make links between them. (3Rf9)

● Make a record of information drawn from a text, e.g. by completing a chart. (3Wn4)

Photocopiable pages 161 and 165; a range of information books; internet access; computers for the learners to use one between two.

## Starter

• Distribute a range of information books on the same subject to the learners in pairs.

• Give the learners an opportunity to peruse the texts and check off some of the features they should expect to find. (See photocopiable page 161 for examples.)

• Give them a subject area relating to the books and ask them to use what they know about contents and index pages to quickly locate information in one of the books they've been given.

• Explain that this is a skill they will use throughout their lives!

## Main activities

• Ask the learners to work with a partner and together choose a section from one of the information books, for example a section relating to mummification.

• Hand out photocopiable page 165 and ask the learners to read through the text, collecting information to record in the table and adding examples where possible.

• Ask the learners to find a related report text on the internet (for example at www.ancientegypt.co.uk/menu) and then fill in the 'Report from the internet' column.

• Discuss how on the internet, topic or technical words often contain a hyperlink to a definition rather than a list of words in a glossary.

## Plenary

• Give the learners an opportunity to share their findings with another pair of learners.

• Ask: *Did you all agree?*

• Discuss any differences and clarify any misconceptions.

• Finally reflect on the different effects created by the two texts. Ask: *Which is better? Which do you prefer? Why?*

• Tell the learners that as writers we can choose and borrow ideas for our own writing from a variety of sources!

Ask the learners:

● What was similar about the report text in the book and the report text from the internet?

● What were the main differences between the report text in the book and the report text from the internet?

● Which was better at drawing the reader in?

● What is good about collecting information from different sources?

**Support:** Organise these learners to work in a small adult-helper led group for the Starter activity, working at an appropriate pace so that all the learners get an opportunity to take part.

**Extension:** Give these learners the opportunity to use a search engine to source other report texts on the internet.

Name: _____

# Comparing reports

Choose two reports – one from a book and one from the internet – and use this table to compare them.

| | Report from a book | Report from the internet |
|---|---|---|
| Layout – how is the information organised? | | |
| How easy is it to read and find out information? | | |
| What type of information is included – maps, diagrams, writing, and so on? | | |
| Are pictures and diagrams used? | | |
| Is there a glossary? | | |
| Which is better or which would you recommend? | | |

# Making an oral report

## Learning objectives

- Plan main points as a structure for story writing. (3Wf5)
- Make a record of information drawn from a text, e.g. by completing a chart. (3Wn4)
- Use ICT sources to locate simple information. (3Rn7)

## Resources

Photocopiable page 167; a range of topic books about the Ancient Egyptians; internet access.

## Starter

- Explain to the learners that they are going to work in groups to create an oral report about Ancient Egypt (this lesson can easily be adapted for another subject).
- Display an enlarged version of photocopiable page 167 and the collection of books about Egypt. Ask: *How are you going to research information for each section of your report?*
- Elicit from the learners that they don't have to read the books from cover to cover – they can use the contents and index to research specific questions.
- Start with the question: *Where is Egypt?* Model searching through one of the books, finding a map, and writing 'North East Africa' in the space provided.

## Main activities

- Distribute photocopiable page 167 and encourage the learners to work with a partner to collect information to answer the questions, as modelled in the Starter activity.
- Explain how they will use their notes when they present their oral report, so they should include enough detail to make their report interesting but should not write every word down.

- After a few minutes, choose a confident learner to share their notes so far. Model turning the notes into proper sentences.
- Tell the learners to continue by using the books and internet to take brief notes to help them talk about their subject and then practise their report, deciding who is going to say what.

## Plenary

- Ask the pairs of learners to join with another pair and share their oral reports. Give them time to edit their notes and make improvements to their report before pairing with a differing pair and sharing reports again.
- Ask: *What extra information or details did you add after listening to another learner? How could you improve your report next time you tell it?*

## Success criteria

Ask the learners:

- What is an oral report?
- How did the questions help organise the report?
- How did you make your notes – what did you write down and what did you leave out?
- How did you use your notes to give your oral report?
- How could your oral report be improved?

## Ideas for differentiation

**Support:** Ask these learners to focus on one section only to research and prepare to talk about.

**Extension:** Provide these learners with an opportunity to be more creative by imagining they are a reporter or television presenter and interviewer / interviewee.

Name: _____

# Ancient Egyptian report

Use this writing frame to make notes about Ancient Egypt.
Use your notes to give an oral report.

| Geography | Where is Egypt? _____ |
| --- | --- |
| | What is the climate / weather like? _____ |
| | _____ |
| **The Nile** | Why was the Nile so important to the Ancient Egyptians? |
| | _____ |
| | _____ |
| | What happened to the Nile once a year? _____ |
| **Daily life** | What was daily life like for ordinary ancient Egyptians? |
| | _____ |
| | _____ |
| | Where did they live, what jobs did they do, and so on? |
| | _____ |
| | _____ |
| **Pharaohs** | Who were they? _____ |
| | _____ |
| | Why were they so important? _____ |
| | _____ |
| **Pyramids** | What are they? _____ |
| | Who built them? _____ |
| | Who were they for? _____ |
| | What is mummification? _____ |
| | _____ |

# Planning a written report

- Plan main points as a structure for story writing. (3Wf5)
- Consider ways that information is set out on page and on screen, e.g. lists, charts, bullet points. (3Rn4)

Photocopiable pages 167 (completed) and 169; large pieces of paper; scissors.

## Starter

- Divide the class into three teams and play a quick game to remind the learners about the features of a report text: Ask each team of learners, one at a time, what features they would expect to find in a report text. Give one point for each correct answer.

## Main activities

- Show the learners an enlarged version of photocopiable page 169 and a filled-in version of photocopiable page 167.
- Explain to the learners how they are going to use the notes they made for the oral report and some or all of the pictures to create a plan for a report text about the Ancient Egyptians.
- Model cutting out the pictures from photocopiable page 169 and arranging them in your preferred order on a large piece of paper. Encourage the learners to be discerning about their choice – they don't have to include all the drawings!
- Continue to model the planning process, using the information from your filled-in photocopiable page 167 to annotate the pictures with notes.
- Hand out individual copies of photocopiable page 169 and large pieces of paper to each learner and ask them to begin to plan their report.

- If the learners have previously worked with a partner then they can continue to do so, but both the learners need to produce a plan for their report.
- Interrupt the learners from time to time to re-focus them on making decisions about which pictures to include and how to incorporate them into the report, rather than just saying 'here's a picture of a pyramid'!

## Plenary

- Provide the learners with an opportunity to display their plan to the rest of the class with a table-top display.
- Ask the learners to feed back on:
  - what they have seen that is good
  - which ideas they would like to 'borrow' from someone else.
- Give the learners time to make brief notes and changes to their plans while the ideas are still fresh in their minds.

Ask the learners:

- What information should go first?
- How did you order your pictures and information?
- Which features of a report have you included?
- How will the pictures help make the report better or more engaging?

**Support:** Ask these learners to choose two or three pictures and focus their report on them.

**Extension:** Encourage these learners to include additional information not covered in the planning table or pictures.

# Illustrations for an Ancient Egyptian report

Collect information about the aspects of Ancient Egyptian life shown in these pictures. Cut out the pictures and use them in your report.

# Writing a report text

- Consider ways that information is set out on page and on screen, e.g. lists, charts, bullet points. (3Rn4)
- Establish purpose for writing, using features and style based on model texts. (3Wn2)

Photocopiable pages 169 and 171; scissors; non-fiction texts about Egypt (if needed); the learners' completed plans from the previous two lessons.

## Starter

- Discuss with the learners how report texts often include subject-specific vocabulary and technical words. Ask: *Which technical words might appear in the report we are writing?*
- Collect the learners' ideas and display them.
- Distribute photocopiable page 171 to the learners in groups of four.
- Tell the learners to cut out the cards and check they know what they all mean. Provide the learners with non-fiction texts to refer to if necessary.
- Next, tell the learners to make a pile of the cards on the table and take it in turns to take a card. The learner who takes the card has to describe what it means to the other three learners without saying the word. The learner who guesses the word first keeps the card. If none of the three learners can guess the word from the description it gets put back in the pile. Continue until all the cards are used up.

## Main activities

- Explain that the purpose of the game was to familiarise the learners with some of the technical language they may need to use in their report.
- Tell them to look at their plans from photocopiable page 167 and check they have chosen the best words to explain and describe the subject matter, including using technical language.

- Encourage the learners to annotate their plans by adding the subject-specific language and noting where they intend to include pictures, maps or diagrams and bullet points.
- Ask them to start writing their first draft. Tell them to use their annotations around the pictures to write the captions. Provide them with a fresh version of photocopiable page 169.

## Plenary

- Play a game of 'technical vocabulary bingo':
  - Using a set of cards from the Starter activity, briefly describe a word, for example: 'These were the kings or rulers in Ancient Egypt.' If the learners can find the word (Pharaoh) in their report draft then they get a point.
  - Award additional points for any other interesting vocabulary used.

Ask the learners:

- What is technical vocabulary?
- Which technical vocabulary have you included in your report?
- Look at the technical or specific language you have chosen; is a glossary necessary?
- How will the layout of your report attract the reader's attention?

**Support:** Organise these learners to work in a small group with an adult helper when describing the vocabulary in the Starter activity.

**Extension:** Encourage these learners to create a short glossary for the technical vocabulary used in their report.

# Technical vocabulary game

Cut out these words and work with a partner to check their meaning.

| | | |
|---|---|---|
| hieroglyphics | pharaohs | mummification |
| shaduf | scribe | amulet |
| Nile | pyramids | archaeologist |
| artefacts | papyrus | Tutankhamen |

# Editing and improving a report text

## Learning objectives

- Use ICT to write, edit and present work. (3Wp4)
- Listen and respond appropriately to others' views and opinions. (3SL4)
- Consider ways that information is set out on page and on screen, e.g. lists, charts, bullet points. (3Rn4)

## Resources

Photocopiable pages 167 (completed), 169 and 173; the learners' first draft of their report and plans from the previous lessons; access to computers, the internet and word-processing software.

## Starter

- Tell the learners to compare their plans with the first draft of their report. Discuss how there is progression from one to the other.
- Tell the learners that they are going to use the computer to create a final version of their report and that you are going to create a non-fiction book by collecting all the individual reports together.

## Main activities

- Explain that the learners are to work with a partner, sharing a computer and taking turns to read and scribe for each other.
- Distribute photocopiable page 173 to each learner. Ask them to keep this success criteria to hand and continue to check their final draft against it as they are writing. This will encourage them to stay focused rather than just copying across one document to another.
- Encourage the learners to edit, add bullet points, insert pictures, and so on. (They can either leave space to stick in the pictures from photocopiable page 169 or use others sourced from the internet.)

- When the learners are finished and happy with their reports, collect up the pages and, depending on class size, either have them all bound together or create two or three smaller books. In celebration of the created book(s) suggest that the learners loan it / them to the school library to go into the Ancient Egyptian section for other learners to enjoy or refer to, lend it to another class to read or include it in a class display.

## Plenary

- Discuss the success criteria on photocopiable page 173 and ask the learners to explain how they think they did, and how they could improve their reports.
- Finally, ask the learners what information should be on a blurb for the class book and write one together. Compare the shared one with the one the extension group wrote and model editing the shared blurb to get a final copy.

## Success criteria

Ask the learners:

- What improvements did you make in the final draft?
- How have you organised the information to engage the reader?
- How did it help to work with a partner on the final draft?
- Which part of the report are you most proud of?

## Ideas for differentiation

**Support:** Ask these learners to produce one shared final draft, each learner choosing one section to find a picture for and word process.

**Extension:** Task these learners with the responsibility of creating a front and back cover for the class book, to include the writers, a title and a blurb.

Name: _____

# Success criteria
## for a report text

Use this checklist to make sure your report has the correct
features. Ask your partner to check your report too.

| I have included: | Author | Partner |
|---|---|---|
| a heading | | |
| sub-headings | | |
| pictures, maps or diagrams | | |
| labels or captions | | |
| information organised into different sections and paragraphs | | |
| technical words | | |
| How many stars does the report get? | ☆ ☆ ☆ ☆ ☆ | ☆ ☆ ☆ ☆ ☆ |
| How can the report be improved? | | |

# Unit assessment

- How are books organised and displayed in a library? How do you know where to start looking for a book?
- How do the index / contents page / glossary help the reader?
- Name five features you would expect to find in a report text.

- How will you use the layout of your report to attract the reader's attention?
- What does the 'gist' of a text mean? What skill do you use to find the gist of a text? When might you use this skill?

## Summative assessment activities

Observe the learners while they play these games. You will quickly be able to identify those who appear to be confident and those who may need additional support.

### Pairs glossary game

This activity demonstrates the learners' ability to use index pages to search for information as they create a glossary using key or technical vocabulary for a topic. (This activity can easily be adapted to another topic or subject by simply choosing 10–12 key vocabulary words from the topic.)

**You will need:**

Sets of cards from photocopiable page 171; information books about the Ancient Egyptians or internet access; blank cards.

**What to do**

- Organise the learners into pairs and give each pair a set of vocabulary cards from photocopiable page 171. Tell the learners to sort them into alphabetical order.

- Next, ask the learners to use a range of non-fiction books or the internet to generate definitions for each of the words.

- Ask the learners to write their definitions on the blank cards and pair them up with the technical words.

- Tell the learners to shuffle the vocabulary and definition cards together and then place them face down on the table.

- Tell the learners to play a game of pairs, matching each word with its meaning.

### Questions and headings

This activity encourages the learners to think about different subjects and break them down into sections.

**You will need:**

Large pieces of paper and marker pens.

**What to do**

- Ask the learners to work with a partner and suggest possible sub-headings they might use if they were writing report texts for the following subjects:
  - the Olympics
  - athletics
  - farming
  - football.

- Tell the learners to collect their ideas on a large piece of paper and make notes of any questions they would like to investigate about the subject.

- Finally, tell the partners to compare their subheadings and questions with another pair.

Distribute individual copies of photocopiable page 175 and ask the learners to complete the book jacket. Remind them that the cover illustration needs to catch the reader's eye and the blurb needs to catch their imagination. Can they come up with a suitable name for the author?

# Secrets of the Pharaohs

Name: _____

Complete the cover for this book about the Pharaohs. Add:

• a blurb and picture on the back cover • a picture and the author's name on the front cover.

**Secrets of the Pharaohs**

Secrets of the Pharaohs

8 371902 400192

## Reading and enjoying poems

### Learning objectives

- Read aloud with expression to engage the listener. (3Rf2)
- Read a range of story, poetry and information books and begin to make links between them. (3Rf9)
- Practise to improve performance when reading aloud. (3SL6)

### Resources

Photocopiable pages 121, 177 and 178.

### Starter

- Display an enlarged version of photocopiable page 177, arranged so that you only display one poem at a time.
- Read the poems to the learners. Provide them with an opportunity to briefly discuss each one.
- Explain that these types of humorous or funny poems are called limericks and that they follow a pattern. (The pattern will be investigated later in the unit on page 187; for now the learners are simply to enjoy them.)
- Distribute individual copies of photocopiable page 177 and ask the learners to read the poems with a partner. Encourage them to read the poems aloud with a steady pace, as it will make the poem more entertaining.
- Give the learners an opportunity to 'perform' their favourite limerick to another pair.

### Main activities

- Display an enlarged version of photocopiable page 178. Read the first poem together with the learners, pausing briefly to discuss it.
- Encourage the learners to be discerning about what they read by asking them the following questions:
  - *What do you think of the poem – do you like it or dislike it?*
  - *Do any 'pictures' come to mind as you read it?*
  - *Do you notice any patterns?*
  - *Does it entertain? Why?*

- Display an enlarged version of photocopiable page 121 and model filling in the learners' responses to the questions on it.
- Distribute individual copies of photocopiable pages 121 and 178. Tell the learners to work with a partner to read and discuss the second poem together before putting their thoughts down on photocopiable page 121.
- Ask the learners to work with a partner to prepare a performance of any of the poems on photocopiable pages 177 or 178. Tell them to rehearse the poem until they are familiar with the rhymes and rhythm.

### Plenary

- Collect some of the learners' responses to 'My elephant thinks I'm wonderful'.
- Provide an opportunity for the learners to perform their rehearsed poem to the rest of the class.
- Ask them to briefly reflect on the performances. Ask: *What was good in the best performances?*

### Success criteria

Ask the learners:

- What type of poetry have you been reading today?
- Have you read any poems like this before?
- What did you like or dislike about the poems?
- How do humorous poems make you feel?
- What sort of patterns did you notice in the poems?

### Ideas for differentiation

**Support:** Ask these learners to make a collective response to the poems, working with an adult helper.

**Extension:** Encourage these learners to begin a class anthology of funny poems, collecting and making copies of their favourites to go into a book.

# Limericks

## Explosive Tale

There was a volcano called Dot –
once on maps just a minute spot.
But, 'I'm hungry!' Dot grumbled
as her insides rumbled.
'And what's more, I'm feeling quite hot!'

Judith Nicholls

## Family Problems

I have a strange Auntie called Jean.
She's quite tall and thin as a bean.
On bright sunny days,
When she's standing sideways,
Auntie Jean cannot even be seen.

John Kitching

## A Young Man with Wobbly Eyes

A young man with wobbly eyes
used to muddle his g's and his y's.
When he said 'guess'
I guess he meant 'yes'
and 'yugs' was how he said 'guys'.

Michael Rosen

# Humorous poems

## A Shark is a Pet

A shark is a pet

that you don't want to get.

There is nothing less fun
than a shark.

He doesn't have fur.

He won't cuddle or purr,

and he never takes walks in the park.

Instead he just stares

and intensely prepares,

as he circles and waits in the dark,

to nibble your nose

and your fingers and toes,

for his bite is much worse than his bark.

Kenn Nesbitt

## My Elephant Thinks I'm Wonderful

My elephant thinks I'm wonderful.

My elephant thinks I'm cool.

My elephant hangs around
with me

and follows me into school.

My elephant likes the way I look.

He thinks that I'm fun and smart.

He thinks that I'm kind and generous

and have a terrific heart.

My elephant thinks I'm brave and bold.

He's proud of my strength and guts.

But mostly he likes the way I smell.

My elephant thinks I'm nuts.

Kenn Nesbitt

# Why is it funny?

## Learning objectives

- Answer questions with some reference to single points in a text. (3Rf3)
- Consider words that make an impact, e.g. adjectives and powerful verbs. (3Rf7)
- Consider how choice of words can heighten meaning. (3PSV11)

## Resources

Photocopiable pages 177, 178, 180 and 181.

## Starter

- Display an enlarged version of photocopiable page 180 and read the two poems aloud, pausing briefly between them. Ask the learners: *What can you tell me about these poems? What makes them funny?*
- Distribute individual copies of photocopiable page 180 and ask the learners to try reading them with a partner.
- Explain that this type of poem is called a tongue twister. Ask: *Why do you think that is?*
- Let the learners have another go at reading the poems to test what they now know about tongue-twisters! Who can read them the fastest?

## Main activities

- Display photocopiable page 177 and read each limerick to the learners. Ask: *Why are these poems funny?* Discuss possible ideas, for example silly or funny people, silly or funny language, they paint a funny picture in your mind, and so on.
- Display photocopiable page 178 and read the poems together one at a time. Discuss why these poems are funny, for example comparing having a pet cat to having a pet shark, and the idea of a pet elephant thinking its owner is 'cool'.
- Refer back to photocopiable page 180 and talk about why these poems are funny, for example a list of silly and totally random objects, or it's funny trying to say these difficult-to-pronounce combinations of words.

- Elicit from the learners that poems can be funny for many reasons.
- Display and distribute photocopiable page 181 and tell the learners to use the poems they are familiar with (from photocopiable pages 177, 178 and 180) to complete the table; the first example has been done for them.

## Plenary

- Briefly let the learners feed back to a partner. Collect some of their ideas onto the displayed version of photocopiable page 181.
- Discuss with the learners how poets work hard and only choose the best words to get their message across, often writing and rewriting their poems, trying out various words. Ask the learners to feed back their favourite line or phrase from all the poems they have read. Ask: *Why do you like it?*

## Success criteria

Ask the learners:

- How and why are these poems funny?
- Which poem is your favourite? Why do you like it?
- Which words and phrases stick out the most?
- What made you giggle the most? Why did it make you giggle?
- What sort of pictures does your favourite poem paint in your mind?

## Ideas for differentiation

**Support:** Ask these learners to complete the table for three poems only and then practise reciting one of the tongue-twisters.

**Extension:** Encourage these learners to search for other funny poems on the internet.

# Tongue-twisters

**Shop Chat**

My shop stocks:

locks, chips,

chopsticks,

watch straps,

traps, tops,

taps, tricks,

ship's clocks,

lipstick and chimney pots.

What does your shop stock?

*Sharkskin socks.*

Libby Houston

**Toboggan**

To begin to toboggan, first buy a toboggan,

But don't buy too big a toboggan.

(A too big a toboggan is not a toboggan

To buy to begin to toboggan.)

Colin West

*Cambridge Primary: Ready to Go Lessons for English Stage 3* © Hodder & Stoughton Ltd 2013

Name: _____

# What makes a poem funny?

Poems can be funny for many different reasons.
Use this table to collect your ideas about why different poems are funny.

| Name of poem: | Nonsense words | Tongue-twisters | Limericks | Silly things happening | Something else ... |
|---|---|---|---|---|---|
| Toboggan | Toboggan is an unusual word and fun to say. | It's hard to read quickly! | | | Repeating the words to, too and toboggan! |
| Shop chat | | | | | |
| My elephant thinks I'm wonderful | | | | | |
| | | | | | |
| | | | | | |

# Performing a poem

**Learning objectives**

● Read aloud with expression to engage the listener. (3Rf2)

● Practise to improve performance when reading aloud. (3SL6)

● Begin to adapt movement to create a character in drama. (3SL7)

**Resources**

Photocopiable pages 183 and 184.

## Starter

• Discuss with the learners that you are going to read them a poem that has been written for two voices. Ask: *What does that mean?* Explain that the poem is like a conversation or dialogue, with one character responding to what the other is saying and doing.

• Read aloud the poem on photocopiable pages 183 and 184 with an adult helper.

• Ask: *Who do the two voices belong to?* (Pet owner and pet.)

• Ask: *Why is the poem funny?* (The owner is misinterpreting the behaviour of his pet dog. They see the same events from very different points of view.)

• Once the learners have an understanding of the poem and how it works, distribute photocopiable pages 183 and 184 and encourage the learners to work with a partner to rehearse the poem for a performance.

## Main activities

• After a short time, interrupt the learners and discuss what they think the success criteria for a 'good' poetry performance should be, for example:
   • 'I practised so I sounded confident.'
   • 'I added actions / props / musical instruments.'
   • 'I acted well and spoke clearly to my audience.'
   • 'I changed my voice by reading quickly / slowly or loudly / softly.'
   • 'I was pleased with my performance and I worked well in a group.'

• 'The audience enjoyed the performance.' (*How do you know?*)
• 'I would give my performance ... stars.'
• 'To improve my performance next time I could ...'
• Are there any other things to remember when performing a poem?

## Plenary

• Give some of the groups of learners an opportunity to perform their poem, and begin modelling feedback on the performance using the success criteria, for example: *Well done – you sounded confident and I could clearly hear every word* or: *You used the volume and speed of your voice to keep the listeners interested.*

• Encourage the learners to continue giving feedback to each other in a similar way.

• Finally, discuss the performances using the success criteria. Ask: *What changes could you make to your performance?*

**Success criteria**

Ask the learners:

● How did the performance go? What went well? What could be improved for next time?

● Why is it important to speak clearly when performing a humorous poem?

● What strategies did you use to engage the listener?

● How did you use your voice?

● How can you tell if the audience enjoyed the performance?

**Ideas for differentiation**

**Support:** Ask these learners to choose a shorter poem or perform the poem choral style using two readers for each 'voice'.

**Extension:** Give these learners an opportunity to use musical instruments or props to support their performance.

# The Dark Avenger

**For two voices**

My dog is called The Dark Avenger.
*Hello, I'm Cuddles.*

She understands every word I say.
*Woof?*

Last night I took her for a walk.
*Woof! Walkies! Let's go!*

Cleverly, she kept 3 paces ahead.
*I dragged him along behind me.*

She paused at every danger, spying out the land.
*I stopped at every lamp-post.*

When the coast was clear, she sped on.
*I slipped my lead and ran away.*

Scenting danger, Avenger investigated.
*I found some fresh chip papers in the bushes.*

I followed, every sense alert.
*He blundered through the trees, shouting, 'Oy, come 'ere! Where are you?'*

Something – maybe a sixth sense – told me to stop.
*He tripped over me in the dark.*

There was a pale menacing figure ahead of us.
*Then I saw the white Scottie from next door.*

# The Dark Avenger (continued)

Avenger sprang into battle, eager to defend her master.
*Never could stand terriers!*

They fought like tigers.
*We scrapped like dogs.*

Until the enemy was defeated.
*Till Scottie's owner pulled him off – spoilsport!*

Avenger gave a victory salute.
*I rolled in the puddles.*

And came back to check I was alright.
*I shook mud over him.*

'Stop it, you stupid dog!'
*He congratulated me.*

Sometimes, even The Dark Avenger can go too far.
*Woof!!*

Trevor Millum

*Cambridge Primary: Ready to Go Lessons for English Stage 3* © Hodder & Stoughton Ltd 2013

# Comparing poems

- Read a range of story, poetry and information books and begin to make links between them. (3Rf9)
- Answer questions with some reference to single points in a text. (3Rf3)

Photocopiable pages 183, 184 and 186; internet access; a tambourine or drum.

## Starter

- This lesson can be adapted for any two funny poems of your choice.
- Read 'The Boneyard Rap' by Wes Magee at www.poetryarchive.org/childrensarchive/singlePoem.do?poemId=382.
- Discuss how this poem is a rap. Ask: *What can you tell me about this poem?* The learners should notice the rhythm and pattern when reading.
- Read the poem to the learners, tapping the beat gently on a drum or tambourine.
- Explain that this poem is ideal for performing. Divide the learners into groups and allocate a verse to each group. Tell the learners to practise reading it choral style (they all read at the same time).
- When the learners are ready, tell them that they will recite the whole poem one group / verse at a time, and you will tap the beat for them to help keep them in time.

## Main activities

- Display enlarged versions of photocopiable pages 183 and 184 and read the poem together, with half the class reading the pet-owner's part and the other half reading the dog's part.

- Now that the learners are familiar with the two poems, begin discussions about them. Ask the learners to think about:
  - how the poets have made the poems funny
  - character descriptions
  - characters' actions
  - use of silly or funny language.
- Display an enlarged version of photocopiable page 186 and distribute individual copies. Tell the learners that they are going to write down what they think about each poem then think about similarities and differences between them.

## Plenary

- Tell the learners to feed back their ideas to the rest of the class.
- Collect the learners' ideas about the poems in a table under the headings 'Similarities' and 'Differences'.
- Ask: *What do you think and feel about the poems?* Provide an opportunity for the learners to make personal responses to what they have read.

Ask the learners:

- What similarities are there between the poems?
- What differences are there between the poems?
- What poetic devices are used in the poems?
- What sort of rhyming patterns do the poems have?
- How did the poems make you feel?

**Support:** Read the poems with these learners before the lesson, ensuring that they are familiar with them.

**Extension:** Tell these learners to work with a partner and to choose a poem each to compare.

Name: _____

# Comparing two poems

Use this table to collect your ideas about two different poems.

| Poem 1 | Poem 2 |
|---|---|
| Title: _____ <br><br> By: _____ | Title: _____ <br><br> By: _____ |
| Likes / dislikes <br><br> _____ <br><br> _____ <br><br> _____ <br><br> _____ | Likes / dislikes <br><br> _____ <br><br> _____ <br><br> _____ <br><br> _____ |
| Effects <br><br> _____ <br><br> _____ <br><br> _____ <br><br> _____ | Effects <br><br> _____ <br><br> _____ <br><br> _____ <br><br> _____ |
| Pictures <br><br> _____ <br><br> _____ <br><br> _____ <br><br> _____ | Pictures <br><br> _____ <br><br> _____ <br><br> _____ <br><br> _____ |
| Patterns <br><br> _____ <br><br> _____ <br><br> _____ | Patterns <br><br> _____ <br><br> _____ <br><br> _____ |

*Cambridge Primary: Ready to Go Lessons for English Stage 3* © Hodder & Stoughton Ltd 2013

# Planning a poem

- Write and perform poems, attending to the sound of words. (3Wf9)
- Choose and compare words to strengthen the impact of writing, including noun phrases. (3Wf10)
- Establish purpose for writing, using features and style based on model texts. (3Wn2)

Photocopiable pages 177 and 188; different-coloured marker pens; rhyming dictionaries.

## Starter

- Display an enlarged version of photocopiable page 177 (or other favourite limericks). Remind the learners that this type of poem is called a limerick. Ask: *What can you tell me about limericks?* Elicit from the learners that limericks have a specific syllable and rhyming pattern:
  - Syllable pattern of 8, 8, 6, 6, 8 (usually)
  - Rhyming pattern of: A, A, B, B, A
- Ask the learners to check this by counting the syllables on each line. Annotate this onto the displayed version to make the point clear.
- Take two different-coloured marker pens and circle the rhyming words to emphasise the rhyming pattern.
- Conclude that in order for it to be a limerick a poem must follow these rules.

## Main activities

- Explain to the learners that they are going to have a go at writing their own limericks about a funny character that they make up.
- Give the learners five minutes to think of a funny character; tell them to think of:
  - descriptions – what the character looks like
  - actions – how they move or behave
  - habits – what they do.
- Distribute photocopiable page 188 and model thinking of a silly character and what they do and noting it on the planning table. Show the learners how to adapt the examples on the table for their own limerick.

- Explain that they must follow the rhythm and rhyme limerick 'rules' from the Starter for their limerick.
- Provide rhyming dictionaries to support the learners' language choices.

## Plenary

- Give the learners some time to share and compare their ideas and plans in small groups.
- Ask: *How did you get on?* Discuss any problems, tricky lines, words they can't find rhymes for, and so on.
- Tell the learners to focus on the 'rules' only – the number of syllables per line and the correct rhyming pattern – when reading each other's poems. Encourage them to be supportive and encouraging towards each other.

Ask the learners:

- What can you tell me about limericks?
- How did you make your limerick funny?
- How can you recognise a limerick? What features should you find?
- How did you use a rhyming dictionary when you planned your limerick?

**Support:** Ask these learners to use the existing limericks from photocopiable page 177 and substitute the rhyming words with new rhyming words.

**Extension:** Challenge these learners to create two or three different limericks using the planning table to explore as many of their ideas as possible.

Name: _____

# Planning a limerick

Use this table to plan your own limerick.
Make sure you have the right number of syllables in each line.
Use the ideas in the table to get you started.

| Some ideas | Your ideas |
|---|---|
| **Line 1 (8 syllables):**<br>There once was a …<br>There was a young man from …<br>I have a strange uncle called … | |
| **Line 2 (8 syllables):**<br>Who decided to …<br>She never …<br>Who ate nothing but … | |
| **Line 3 (6 syllables):**<br>When the weather was …<br>If you looked in his eye<br>When he opened his mouth | |
| **Line 4 (6 syllables):**<br>He yelled out …<br>Her pet cat …<br>The plate dropped and smashed! | |
| **Line 5 (8 syllables):**<br>He never went down there again!<br>It was a shame, but …<br>No one else would take any blame! | |

*Cambridge Primary: Ready to Go Lessons for English Stage 3* © Hodder & Stoughton Ltd 2013

# Editing and improving a poem

## Learning objectives

- Write and perform poems, attending to the sound of words. (3Wf9)
- Choose and compare words to strengthen the impact of writing, including noun phrases. (3Wf10)
- Establish purpose for writing, using features and style based on model texts. (3Wn2)

## Resources

Photocopiable pages 188 (completed) and 190; dictionaries; thesauruses.

## Starter

- Divide the learners into small groups and give each group a list of words. Tell the groups to come up with as many rhyming words as they can for the words on their list, for example: 'log' – 'slob', 'yob', 'dog', 'blog'; 'eating' – 'beating', 'seating', 'greeting', 'meeting', and so on.
- Share the lists, discussing any unusual / made-up words. Explain that poets do sometimes make up words – it's called using artistic licence!

## Main activities

- Remind the learners that, as they have seen, poems are not always very long. Consequently, poems are filled with very carefully chosen vocabulary.
- Ask: *How can we find a better word to use?* Choosing the 'best' word is often by trial and error – swapping in one word and re-reading to see if it sounds better.
- Ask the learners to get out their plans for their limericks (photocopiable page 188), and read their limerick as it stands so far.
- Encourage the learners to use dictionaries and thesauruses to improve the vocabulary in their limerick, discussing their word choices with a partner using questions such as: 'Can you think of a better word than "big" that I could use here?' or 'I need a word to rhyme with "white". Can you think of one?'

- Ask the learners to share some of their improved ideas with the rest of the class.
- Distribute photocopiable page 190 and discuss the success criteria for their humorous poem.
- Give the learners an opportunity to make any final changes to their limerick in view of the success criteria then to write up their final draft. These could be word-processed and used to create a shared anthology of limericks.

## Plenary

- Ask the learners to read their own poem or each other's poems in groups. Remind them that poetry is very personal – the poet will have taken a great deal of time and effort so the listeners must show respect.
- When the learners have heard each other's poems they can decide on one from each group to perform to the whole class, read either by the writer or by you.

## Success criteria

Ask the learners:

- Is your poem funny and entertaining? Explain why. What strategies did you use?
- Explain any patterns in your poem.
- How did your choice of words help make the poem funny?
- How did you enrich your vocabulary choices?

## Ideas for differentiation

**Support:** Put these learners into mixed-ability groups for the Starter.

**Extension:** Ask these learners to select a small number of poems for the class anthology based on the success criteria.

Name: _____

# Success criteria for a humorous poem

Check your poem against the success criteria below to make sure it is the best it can be. Ask your partner to check your poem too.

| Success criteria | Poet | Partner |
|---|---|---|
| I wrote a funny poem about: | | |
| It was funny because: | | |
| There was a rhyming pattern. | | |
| I swapped these words to make the poem better: | | |
| I read it clearly so my audience could hear every word. | | |
| It made the listener laugh. | | |
| Next time I would ... | | |
| How many stars would you give the poem? | ☆ ☆ ☆ ☆ ☆ | ☆ ☆ ☆ ☆ ☆ |

*Cambridge Primary: Ready to Go Lessons for English Stage 3 © Hodder & Stoughton Ltd 2013*

# Unit assessment

- Which poems did you enjoy reading? Why?
- How did it feel to perform a poem? What advice would you give someone who was about to perform a poem?

- Explain why some poems are funny.
- Which poems made you laugh the most?
- Are poems better read aloud or inside your head? Try to explain why.

## Summative assessment activities

Observe the learners while they play these games. You will quickly be able to identify those who appear to be confident and those who may need additional support.

### Limerick juggle

This activity allows the learners to demonstrate their ability to think creatively about rhyming words and make choices about altering their vocabulary choices for the best effect.

**You will need:**

Photocopiable page 177.

**What to do**

- Ask the learners to work in groups and give each group photocopiable page 177.
- Tell the learners to choose one of the poems and to work together to rewrite it in a different way. Explain that they can change the rhyming words, information about the character or the subject, and so on, but they must keep the following rhyme and syllable pattern:
  - rhyming pattern: A, A, B, B, A
  - syllable pattern: 8, 8, 6, 6, 8 (if possible).
- When the learners have finished they can share their new version of the limerick with the rest of the group and compare the sorts of changes they made.

### Mouth aerobics

This activity allows the learners to demonstrate their ability to make careful vocabulary choices to create phrases or sets of words suitable for a tongue-twister poem.

**You will need:**

Photocopiable page 180; large pieces of paper; dictionaries, thesauruses and rhyming dictionaries.

**What to do**

- Ask the learners to work in pairs and give each pair photocopiable page 180 and a large piece of paper and access to dictionaries, thesauruses and rhyming dictionaries.
- Tell them to read the poems on photocopiable page 180 to remind themselves how much fun tongue-twisters are.
- Challenge them to work together to create some ideas for tongue-twister lines or phrases. Explain that they don't need to be all for the same poem. Encourage them to 'borrow' ideas from tongue-twisters they have read and use rhyming dictionaries and thesauruses to add to this list or create new ones. They can collect their words on the large piece of paper.
- What's the longest string of alliterative words they can come up with?

Provide the learners with photocopiable pages 183 and 184. Ask them to read the poem again and complete the comprehension on page 192, working individually.

Name: _____

# The Dark Avenger

Read the poem 'The Dark Avenger' and answer these questions:

1.  Who is the Dark Avenger and is that a good name for him?

    _____

    _____

2.  Give two reasons why this poem is funny.

    a)  _____

    b)  _____

3.  What do you think the owner thinks of his dog?

    _____

    _____

4.  What do you think the dog thinks of his owner?

    _____

    _____

5.  This is a poem for two voices. Explain what that means.

    _____

    _____

6.  Think about how the dog is described in the poem and draw a picture of either the Dark Avenger or Cuddles.

*Cambridge Primary: Ready to Go Lessons for English Stage 3* © Hodder & Stoughton Ltd 2013